D1172788

UNDERSTANDING YOUR DOG

Books by Dr. Michael W. Fox

Inhumane Society: The American Way of Exploiting Animals
Superdog
The New Eden
Agricide: The Hidden Crisis That Affects Us All
The New Animal Doctor's Answer Book
The Whistling Hunters
Behavior of Wolves, Dogs, and Related Canids
One Earth, One Mind
Farm Animals; Husbandry, Behavior and Veterinary Practice
The Healing Touch
Dr. Michael Fox's Massage Program for Cats and Dogs
Love is a Happy Cat
How to Be Your Pet's Best Friend
Returning to Eden: Animal Rights and Human Responsibility
The Soul of the Wolf
Understanding Your Pet
Between Animal and Man: The Key to the Kingdom
Understanding Your Dog
Understanding Your Cat
Concepts in Ethology, Animal and Human Behavior
Integrative Development of Brain and Behavior in the Dog

Books Edited by Dr. Michael W. Fox

The Wild Canids
On The Fifth Day: Animal Rights and Human Ethics
The Dog: Its Domestication and Behavior
Readings in Ethology and Comparative Psychology
Abnormal Behavior in Animals
Advances in Animal Welfare Science

Children's Books

Animals Have Rights Too
The Way of the Dolphin
The Touchlings
Lessons From Nature: Fox's Fables
Whitepaws: A Coyote-Dog
Wild Dogs Three
What Is Your Dog Saying?
Ramu and Chennai
Sundance Coyote
The Wolf
Vixie, The Story of a Little Fox

UNDERSTANDING

Everything You Want to Know About Your D

YOUR DOG

but Haven't Been Able to Ask Him

Michael W. Fox

D.Sc., Ph.D., MRCVS

St. Martin's Griffin
New York

Library of Congress Cataloging-in-Publication Data

Fox, Michael W.
    Understanding your dog / Michael W. Fox.
      p.   cm.
    ISBN 0-312-07108-6 (pbk.)
    I. Title.
  SF433.F685 1992
  636.7'0887—dc20   91-39314
                                                CIP

First published in the United States by Coward, McCann & Geoghegan, Inc.

First U.S. Paperback Edition: March 1992
10 9 8 7 6 5 4 3 2

To Deanna and Loppy

Acknowledgments

Some of the material in this book has been published earlier in part in *Dogs* magazine, Countrywide Publications, New York. The author is especially grateful to Herm David, past editor of *Dogs* and an authority on dogs himself, for his encouragement and advice in preparing this book. The research was in part supported by a grant to the author from the Center for the Biology of Natural Systems, Washington University.

Contents

Foreword

This book is designed to provide the reader with a deeper
knowledge of the behavior of the dog, a species which, by virtue
of its close association with man for several thousand years, is
closer to the heart and mind than any other domesticated
animal. It is intended as a learning experience for dog owner,
breeder and trainer and contains material that gives the serious
student of canine behavior a concrete basis for really getting
inside the dog's mind as well as objectively understanding the
nature and social behavior of the animal. What better learning
experience for children than to follow the gradual unfolding of a
newly acquired puppy's behavior and for them to understand his
basic needs by knowing how he talks and what his actions mean.
To understand—to be "inside" or "at one" with an animal—to
comprehend and predict his motives and actions is an enriching
experience, and a person without such insight is missing a big
hunk of life.

Much has been written on the canine psyche, on the
astonishing abilities of certain dogs, some bordering on extrasensory perception, others explainable in more rational terms.
And the fidelity, intelligence and remarkable capacities of the
dog to perform truly incredible feats have been celebrated by

poet, novelist and journalist. It is difficult to separate fact from fancy in many of their accounts, and the subjective emotional meanderings of some imaginative authors elevate the dog to the status of man himself. In this book, the information is derived from years of patient and disciplined research and opens the doors of perception to bring the reader to a closer understanding of the dog and perhaps to a deeper understanding of all living things, including mankind.

It's surprising how little has been written about the behavior of the dog, except where such knowledge is of practical importance for handling and training dogs or for show, guard duty or various field sports. Available information is scattered and represents only a few areas of purely applied interest. In this book we start at the beginning, observing how a young animal matures, develops new behavior patterns and learns to communicate with its own species and with man.

A concise picture of some of the fascinating changes that occur in the brain and behavior of the dog as it matures is presented, with particular emphasis on how experiences early in life can have profound effects on later behavior. Several experiments which have been conducted to test the validity of certain routine practices in dog rearing are described, and the results of these experiments are of considerable practical importance. Understanding how your dog grows and learns will afford a greater understanding of man's closest companion and also a deeper insight into the whys and wherefores, dos and don'ts of dog rearing and handling.

Introduction

It gives me great pleasure to write an introduction to this reissue of *Understanding Your Dog,* since it has already helped one generation of dog owners and several generations of dogs from the time that it was first published in 1974.

Animals are a constant in our lives and they do not change from one generation to the next. But language does change, so the reader should forgive such outdated "sexist" overtones as my use of the term man and mankind, instead of people and humanity. However, in spite of changes in word usage and in our attitudes and values, the facts about dog behavior in this book remain unchanged because dogs, more ancient than we, will always be dogs.

As a veterinarian, I feel that this book makes a significant contribution to helping improve the health and well-being of our canine companions. This is because the better we understand them, the better we can care for them. Love without understanding is not enough.

As an animal behaviorist (or ethologist) and as an advocate of animal rights and protection, I am convinced that progress in the humane treatment of animals comes first, not through laws, but through a change in our attitudes and values through understanding animals' behavior, development, social and emotional needs. Such understanding leads to a greater respect and reverence for all creatures and a deeper communion with all of creation.

It also means a more fulfilling relationship with our animal companions and to this end, I dedicate my book.

—DR. MICHAEL W. FOX
Washington, D.C., 1991

UNDERSTANDING YOUR DOG

1

Origin and History of the Dog:
Wolf-Dog or Man-Dog?

AT ONE TIME it was thought that God created man, and the notion and supporting evidence that man actually evolved from the apes was morally and socially unacceptable. Although God did not create man per se, man certainly had a hand in creating dog. With the capacity for culture, man became increasingly capable of determining his own destiny. He gained greater control over the environment by developing agriculture and over many animals by domesticating them. The more he came to dominate nature, the more arrogant, conceited and detached he became from nature, until he regarded himself as created apart from the rest of the world. An apelike ancestry was inconceivable. But times have now changed and man is looking into his past and studying animals in order to comprehend more fully his own nature and evolutionary past.

Man, to a degree, created dog, not always in his own image, but in form and temperament most suited to various utilitarian purposes. God did not create all men equal in the genetic sense. Various races evolved, each neither superior nor inferior to the others but different and uniquely adapted physically and culturally to a particular environment. Neither did man create dog equal. He selected various types differing in size, strength, stamina, aggression and trainability. Each type was superbly fitted to a particular task or role, neither superior nor inferior to other specialist breeds but different and uniquely adapted. But the mystery remains as to the origin of the dog prior to man's intervention, and in this chapter this mystery will be explored and some of the consequences of domestication will be discussed.

The modern breeds of domesticated dog belong to the family Canidae along with their wild cousins, the wolves, coyotes, jackals and foxes. They are all flesh-eaters, or carnivores, but unlike the other carnivores such as the cats, which mainly ambush their prey, they instead chase after and run down their prey. Consequently members of the dog family are characteristically built for speed and endurance. Some species, such as the fox, are solitary hunters, while others, like the wolf, hunt in packs. The wolf type is therefore very sociable.

Dr. L. H. Colbert has traced the ancestry of the dog from fossil remains of various carnivores, going back as far as the transition from the Eocene to the Oligocene ages, some 40,000,000 years ago. A small, civetlike carnivorous animal lived during this period which has been given the name *Miacis*. Present-day civets are possibly his direct descendants. Later in the Oligocene, two species emerged from *Miacis*, one a bear-dog or wolverinelike animal from which the present-day bears are believed to have evolved. The other offshoot, known as *Cynodictis*, is thought to be the grandfather of all the dog family.

Cynodictis apparently had partially retractile claws and therefore most probably lived in trees. From this, in the lower Miocene, arose two more evolutionary branches, one giving rise to the present-day hunting dogs of India and Africa. The other, *Cynodesmus*, which developed into large hyenalike animals, was destined to become extinct in North America. But during the upper Miocene the offshoot of *Cynodesmus* evolved, *Tomarctus*, from which the wolf, dog and fox are thought to have evolved.

In spite of the common ancestry of present-day carnivorous mammals, the origin of the domesticated dog is clouded in the unrecorded history of primitive man. Our only recourse is to sift through archeological remains. Careful excavations have shown that for at least the last 10,000 years man has had dogs as close companions. Examination of the skulls of the animals has revealed that they were indeed dogs and that the only wild animal with comparable dental characteristics is the wolf.

Some relatives of the domesticated dog: (top left) New Guinea Singing dog, which is the same species as domesticated dogs but which, like the Australian Dingo, may be an ancient domesticated breed that contributed to many more recent breeds; (top right) Mexican wolves; (bottom left) so-called Texas "red wolves," these are almost extinct and many specimens may be half coyote or dog; (bottom right) a second-generation coyote-beagle hybrid. Dogs will crossbreed with wolves, coyotes and jackals

Jackals, coyotes and foxes have much less in common with the dog in terms of skeletal features, even though the jackal and coyote will interbreed with the domesticated dog. The consensus is, then, that the wolf is the closest cousin of the domesticated dog. Some authorities contend that the dog is directly descended from the wolf, while others believe that the present-day dog is the descendant of wolf crossed with a close relative which was more doglike than wolflike in appearance. This "missing link" may be a dingo or basenjilike ancestor. But when we look at the worldwide distribution of the wolf and the regional variations in body size and coat color, it is not difficult to imagine that thousands of years ago orphaned wolf cubs were raised by primitive man, who selected only those with the most stable temperament and other attributes desirable in an animal that guards the home or other domesticated livestock or assists its master on hunting expeditions.

The complex cycle of the evolution of dog breeds which parallels the evolution and spread of human cultures makes it difficult to go back in time and determine the origins of the many breed types. Some types, like the American Indian dogs, came with their migrant human companions, and we can trace their route from their native land by the close similarities in the now geographically isolated breeds. But where did these original dogs come from? From one center, such as Mesopotamia (and also Asia and Europe as a secondary source), or perhaps from several places at different times?

The dog was a very valuable commercial item, and as transportation improved and regional and international trade increased there was a breakdown in the geographic isolation of many breeds. They were gradually disseminated throughout the civilized world. Perhaps an indication of a high degree of cultural sophistication is the great diversity of indigenous breeds, notably the emergence of so many breeds from the major classes of dogs in England, which have changed little since the seventeenth century (see later).

Mesopotamia, a region of great cultural evolution 2,000 years

B.C., was probably the major source of domesticated dogs of various types that were gradually disseminated throughout Asia and Europe in later years. The saluki and the Kurdish herding dog, which resembles the large mastifflike hunting and war dogs depicted in Babylonian art, are two of the most ancient breeds from this Mesopotamian source. It is quite probable that dogs of these two types—coursing, "eye" hunting, greyhound type and heavier-bodied guard and war dogs—were traded and bred with indigenous European dogs to increase the diversity of breeds and the potential usefulness of new breeds or hybrid combinations, which if successful were standardized by careful selective breeding.

DOGS OF AMERICAN INDIANS

According to Glover Allen, Harvard zoologist and anthropologist, the dogs of the early American Indians were brought from Asia with their migrating human companions. He doubts if crossbreeding with indigenous wolves or coyotes had much, if any, influence on the original stock. Allen recognized three distinct types of dogs among the American aborigines: (1) a large, broad-muzzled Eskimo dog, with heavy coat and tail curled over the hip, and (2) a larger and (3) a smaller Indian dog from which are derived several distinct local breeds. The Eskimo dog is a type common to northern Asia and Europe and doubtless reached America with the Eskimos, whose arrival in eastern America is relatively recent. The Eskimo dog will mate with wolves and produce fertile offspring. Such occurrences may have been accidental or sometimes done experimentally to improve the domesticated stock. The Malemute and Husky are in many ways more wolflike than other breeds (the German shepherd is more a mimic of the wolf—a sheep dog in wolf's clothing). Allen draws an interesting parallel between the two large and small types of American Indian dogs and the two groups of prehistoric European dogs—one large (*Canis intermedis*) and the other small (*Canis palustris*)—which were abundant in the late Neolithic and early Bronze ages. The obvious probability is that these two general types of dogs were widely cultivated in Asia and at a very early period reached Europe and America with human immigrants.

Many "local" breeds of the large and small American Indian dogs were recognized, each geographically isolated tribe having its own particular breed. This must have been so at earlier times in Asia and Europe, before trade and travel reduced local variations. Local breeds became "contaminated" with imported stock, so that local differences were reduced and regional similarities emerged. Succession may also have occurred; for example, the Caucasian American has imported most of the present-day European and Asiatic breeds and has favored very few of the local breeds of the American Indian (Eskimo dog and Chihuahua and Mexican hairless, for example).

OLDE ENGLISH DOGGES

In England in the sixteenth century, Caius, a professor at Cambridge University, wrote an informative paper on the various dog breeds present in the country at that time. The following were recognized: the now extinct silent poacher's dog (the "thievish" dog), rabbit-hunting "tumbler" and "lyemmer." He described several terriers (from the French *terre*, or ground) which were used to drive foxes and badgers from their earths. "Spanielles" (possibly from Spain) were used especially for hunting birds with nets. The dogs would either stalk and flush the birds into a net or more usually silently display where the birds were hiding in the grass and crouch low to allow the net to be thrown over them and hopefully onto the birds. Caius also described setters, which were also used to net birds. They would either point them or creep low and slowly toward them, remain silent and, on command, flush the birds into the net. Scent hounds, with pendulous ears and lips, were also evident in the sixteenth century, including bloodhounds, swift or "gase hounds" and greyhounds that course after large animals such as deer. Shepherd dogs, large mastifflike guard dogs, and

Dogs have been part of man's culture for as far back as archeological records will take us. Here, Chihuahua-like fighting dogs are depicted in Aztec pottery, (*circa* A.D. 200). Others were fattened on corn and eaten as a delicacy

spaniellike lap dogs (King Charles spaniel type) were also abundant. Richard Blome, in a book published some one hundred years later, added to Caius' list with the "lurcher," used for rabbit hunting, and also described the "land spaniels" that were trained to search for birds and then lie still as the net was dragged over them and the birds secured. It is possible that new breeds arose with the advent of the shotgun. Springer spaniels were developed to flush or spring birds from cover, others were trained to point—the pointers—and others to settle in a low point to indicate where the birds were hiding—the setters. It is remarkable to see how well these abilities are stamped into these particular breeds. Young, naive setters and pointers show an immediate interest in small game. It is this general phenomenon—the presence of particular traits which emerge early in life and which are easily accessible to training and are not buried or otherwise inhibited by conflicting traits such as giving voice or rushing forward when excited—that determine their value as sporting dogs. Retrievers were also a later development, as the gun replaced the net, the arrow and the hawk.

The consensus is that most of the present-day breeds are interrelated, arising at some time in the past from crossbreeding. For example, Blome observed that a good "terrier dog" comes from mating a beagle hound with a mastiff-type mongrel or guard dog. As dogs spread from province to province, adaptive radiation was facilitated, in that new populations arose from a few variable, colonizing individuals.

EARLY DOMESTICATION

But how did the dog actually become domesticated? Current theory holds that the smallest of the wolves, the Asiatic wolf, *Canis lupus pallipes*, is the dog's original ancestor. But there was so much folklore surrounding the wolf that to take a wolf cub as a potential companion would be the last thing a sane tribesman would have done. More likely he would have let his children play with it if it was not yet overfearful, and later he would have eaten it or, to appease the gods (or wolf spirits), either sacrificed or released it some distance from his home. Normally, even if it has been hand-reared from an early age, a wolf's wild temperament appears. It is not aggressive but more fearful and wary of unfamiliar stimuli. But there are exceptional wolves that do not develop this temperamental wariness to the same degree as most of their littermates. Perhaps a tribesman might have tamed one of these and raised it into adulthood. A neighbor might have had a wolf of the opposite sex and of similar temperament, and so eventually a litter was born. This may have been the way in which wild animals were first domesticated. Stable temperaments and tractability were selected for over successive generations, and any cubs showing signs of the "wild" temperament were destroyed. These practices, coupled with taming or socializing of suitable pups by gentle handling and constant exposure to people, were later followed up with training to perform certain tasks.

As soon as a reliable temperament was "fixed" in the local breed, the descendants of the original tribesman might have then concentrated on selecting for other traits—either enhancing or reducing certain wolf behavior. Wolves only occasionally bark, but they do have the capacity, and the tribesman might have selected those cubs that barked more readily for guarding the village or hut and, given the choice, would have chosen the smallest barker in the litter for his hut. The silent offspring, on the other hand, might have been trained as hunters, for barking could warn the prey and give it plenty of time for escape. Some might only give voice when they had the prey cornered or were close on its trail; the hunter could then easily find his canine companion and quickly dispatch the cornered or exhausted prey. Wolves run in packs and cooperate in hunting. Several tribesmen, each with his own canid companion, could unite into one large hunting party, using this behavior to advantage. Selective breeding might even have enhanced some of the capacities of the wolf ancestor, who hunted more by eye than by nose or ear. It would have been advantageous to select and train offspring for work in dense cover to hunt more by nose and ear.

In contrast to the domesticated packs of hunting dogs that show a good deal of mutual tolerance, it was less important for the guard and house dogs to retain a high degree of such tolerance and of allelomimetic or group-coordinated behavior. Even today, we see how intolerant terriers are of each other, compared to the pack hounds such as the beagle and foxhound.

There is also evidence to suggest that in domesticating the dog from its wolflike ancestor, a high selection priority was placed on docility and submission to all people in some breeds and to only one or a few people in others—*i.e.,* liberal versus conservative or "one-man" types. Konrad Lorenz at one time thought that these two types reflected a difference in ancestry, one descending from the wolf, the other from the jackal. The jackal ancestry has since been discarded, however, as highly improbable. Suffice it to say at this stage that the one-man type is characteristic of many of the working dogs, notably the guard dogs.

The submissive, all-accepting type is, on the other hand, characteristic of most of the toy breeds and appears to be increasing in occurrence in many breeds that were originally more independent and one-man oriented. The overt behavior of such adult dogs closely resembles the obsequious, submissive behavior of a young pup. Clearly, breeds of this general personality type appear to retain certain infantile behavior patterns. These patterns persist into adulthood and such infantilism may be the combined result of both selective breeding and type of rearing (treating the dog as a perpetual puppy). In addition, many of these breeds show a marked retardation of growth or retention of infantile features—smaller teeth, poorly developed temporal and masseter muscles and a large and often domed puppylike head in proportion to the body. This structural modification in which the development of mature characteristics is reduced or eliminated and infantile features are retained is known as paedomorphosis or neoteny. Indeed, all domesticated animals compared to their wild relatives show varying degrees of neoteny, and in some breeds of dogs the degree is extreme. This combined effect of selective breeding and rearing points to the esthetic and emotional needs that certain toy breeds may be designed to fulfill.

WOLF AND DOG DIFFERENCES

There are other pertinent differences between the wolf and domesticated dog, which most probably arose as a consequence of artificial selection from the foundation stock of early wolflike domestic dogs. A desirable trait for economic reasons is high fertility and early sexual maturity, and these are traits common to most domesticated species. The dog is no exception, for we find in comparing it with the wolf that the latter only has one heat cycle each year and that females attain sexual maturity at two years and the males at three years of age. By comparison, domesticated breeds vary in the age of onset of sexual activity, which may be as early as seven months, and most breeds have two heats per year.

The following basic structural peculiarities are common to many breeds and may represent simple mutations from the wolf ancestor, which were carefully propagated and fixed as characteristics of certain breeds.

1. Pendulous or flop ears (wolf ears are erect).
2. Reduction in body size—miniaturization. Many toy breeds have large craniums in proportion to the rest of the skeleton, indicating that they are derived from a larger ancestor, descendants from which were selected for a smaller body size, but selection for small cranium in proportion tto the body was more difficult to achieve.
3. Curly tail, as in the Spitz group (the wolf tail is held down, as in the German shepherd, in the resting position).
4. Reduction in size of jaws and teeth. Even the large-skulled Saint Bernard has much smaller teeth and jaws than the wolf. Many breeds also have reduced numbers of teeth.
5. Modification of skull: mandible proportions, to produce the brachycephalic (bulldog or pug face) and dolichocephalic

(long-nosed borzoi face) (many breeds are like the wolf—namely mesocephalic).

6. Modification of coat—color, pattern, length of hair and proportion of guard hair to underfur; reduction of season molt (or of molting per se in such breeds as the Afghan hound); reduction of active secretion of tail gland, although some breeds still have a triangle or stripe marking where this atrophied gland lies one-third down the dorsal surface of the tail. Many breeds show the adult coat color at birth, while others, such as the Afghan hound, have a darker "puppy coat" that later molts, yielding the adult pelage and color. (The wolf follows this latter developmental sequence.)

7. Selection for extreme skeletal characteristics—namely, acromegaly, or giantism, as in the deer and elk hound, and dwarfism, or achondroplasia, as in the basset hound.

A problem occasionally encountered by dog breeders is that of mate selection; some bitches show a marked preference for certain males, refusing others, often violently. Males more rarely show preferences; a Shi Tsu from an all golden line refused to breed with black-and-white females when sold as an adult to a kennel with both golden and black-and-white females. But he readily mated with goldens. Such mate preferences are rare in the dog, but in the wolf monogamy is the rule. Clear mate preferences are seen, although social structure within the male and female dominance hierarchies may prevent preferred pairs from mating. It is clearly advantageous to the dog breeder to have promiscuous dogs, so that he, rather than the dogs, can determine who mates with whom. The wolfish trait of monogamy may have been selected against in the propagation of early domesticated dogs, which would explain the promiscuity and indiscriminate matings of the majority of present-day dogs.

As different cultures evolved—those with different hunting techniques, those with different herds of livestock and the more esthetically developed cultures that used smaller dogs for the homestead, hearth or lap—so evolved a wide variety of dogs. Under the intense pressures of artificial selection, a broad spectrum of domesticated dogs emerged, and early on in each province variations within litters were reduced. Local breeds became standardized. Different classes of dogs emerged as valuable commodities for hunting by eye, ear or nose, varying in size according to the size of the prey and in the way they assisted in capturing it by flushing, pointing, retrieving, cornering and killing. Other types were more suited for guarding livestock or the homestead or for light draft work. In some regions, dogs were raised, and still are, for food.

It is easy to imagine that quite early on in the process of domestication and selection wives and children enjoyed the company of the little pups that were destined to become working dogs and that they especially favored undersized "runts" which normally would have been destroyed. As these smaller dogs, or mutants, matured, they became close companions and would at least warn their masters of the presence of any intruders and even frighten them off with their barking. Thus in many regions small house dogs, and later "miniature" and "toy" varieties, became popular, highly prized by the nobility and of status value to the *bourgeoisie*. Today, of course, such types are plentiful, and status of ownership is usually only in the mind of the owner!

The breeds that differed considerably from one province to the next (compare the Scottish terrier with the Skye terrier, Norwich, Manchester, Irish and Welsh terriers) can still be placed in one of four classes by virtue of the fact that they include working dogs (for droving, guarding and light draft work), sporting dogs (pointers, setters and retrievers), terriers (house dogs) and toy or pet dogs.

We see in the evolution of the domesticated dog a clear regional basis for breed origin and cross-cultural or interregional similarities in the class to which a particular breed belongs. From early times, crossbreeding must have contributed significantly to the development of new breeds having the combined attributes of parental stock (the Airedale, for example, is a product of Welsh terrier and Otter hound). At a later stage of domestication and selection a high degree of stability follows as breeds become standardized. Linebreeding and outbreeding to improve a particular strain with the attributes of another line of the same breed are common practices.

DOGS OF TODAY

It is intriguing to look at the present distribution of dog breeds in relation to national and international standards. Western Europe and America essentially predominate in the world arena with large numbers of a few select and standard breeds, and there is mutual exchange between these continents to improve certain lines by outbreeding. In the search for diversity, new standards are being set—not for newly emerging breeds (although "new" breeds such as the Chesapeake Bay retriever and Parson Jack Russell terrier are exceptions) but for long-established regional breeds that are being "discovered" and popularized. The African basenji, Tibetan Lhasa Apso, French Briard, Hungarian Komodonor and Puli and Belgian Bouvier des Flanders.

Few of these breeds emerging from regional and national to international recognition will be used for the purposes for which they were originally bred. Many are used for show alone, and even in some well-established breeds we now see a dichotomy emerging. Show types and field or working types of the same breed are being developed: witness the heavy-boned and muscular field trial Labrador and its more delicate show-ring counterpart. A new breed gains recognition by kennel clubs once sufficient people are actively interested and provided there is a good standardized population of the breed in question. Boston was—and, some say, still is—the most culturally advanced city in the United States, and it was from this nidus that the first original American-bred dog emerged to gain international recognition—namely the Boston terrier.

We do not have the evidence to completely rule out the possibility that at some time and place a jackal or other canid contributed to the genetic foundation of the domesticated dog. As a consequence of the art and science of domestication, where artificial selection can produce remarkable changes within only a

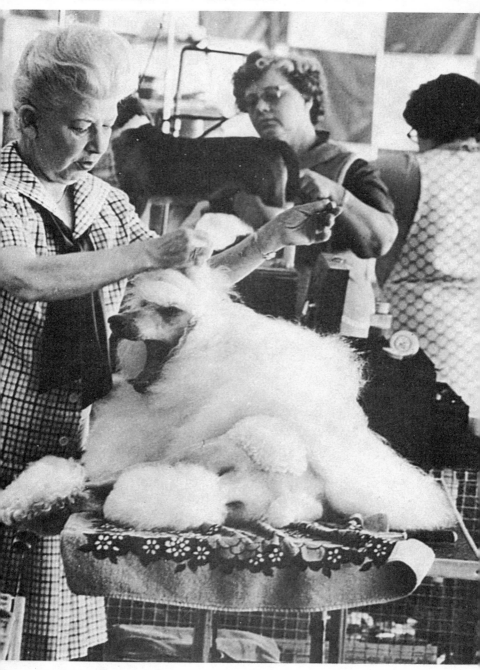

Modern dogs are used for a variety of purposes, some for show . . .

Some for guard work after rigoro[us] training . . .

Some for pointing and retrieving game . . .

Some for the "sport" of fox hunting or
for herding domestic livestock . . .

And some, after months of careful
testing and training, for use as guides
for the blind

few generations, compared to the slow pace of natural selection, we see the great diversity of present-day domesticated dogs. The evidence of 100-percent wolf ancestry of the dog is not as yet conclusive; dogs differ in many ways from wolves, probably not because of a different ancestry, but as a result of domestication and selective breeding. We can conclude therefore that the wolf is the closest wild cousin of the dog and is probably his main progenitor. Some research on behavior genetics in the author's laboratory, as yet only in its early beginnings, promises to reveal some new facts about the origins of the domesticated dog. Working with beagles, coyotes, beagle-coyote hybrids, wolves, Malemutes, and wolf-Malemute hybrids, some behavior patterns which are characteristic of the domesticated dog and of no wild canid, be it wolf or coyote, have been identified. It may well be that the present domesticated dog is derived from a very different ancestor distantly related to the wolf but a distant species long before man began to domesticate dogs.

We no longer have to go into the wild and dig a litter of pups out of their den or go to the next village, famous for its guard dogs, to barter goods for one of its prize animals. Instead, we are literally surrounded by amateur and professional breeders and by good and bad pet stores, and picking up a pup nowadays is an easy matter. But contemporary man can make mistakes, and there are many pitfalls that one should be on the lookout for. In the next chapter, these hazards will be discussed and will serve as a guide for the prospective puppy owner.

2

On Buying a Puppy

CHRISTMAS IS A time for giving, and whatever we buy, we can never be sure that it will be the perfect gift. It's the giving, not the gift, that counts. But there *are* exceptions. The Christmas puppy. You may buy it as a gift for your child or for a close friend or relative. Think again. It is not simply a commodity but a small creature that needs considerable attention. The puppy is a responsibility. Countless numbers of Christmas and other gift puppies die or finish up at the local humane society or in a foster home, if they are lucky.

I want to discuss briefly some of the problems not only of Christmas puppies but also of puppies that are purchased at any time of the year from large department or chain pet stores. Although a cute, playful puppy in his cage may seem completely healthy and full of bounce, he might have been stressed very recently and now be incubating a disease that could flare up in a few days—those few days after you have bought him and taken him home.

Any animal reacts to the stress of being crated and shipped. The reaction will be more intense if its experiences while in transit to pet or department store are physiologically and psychologically traumatic. Cold, vibration, inadequate food and water and the fear of being confined can have an ominous combined effect. A puppy's stress reaction is a defense mechanism, involving the production of certain hormones from the adrenal glands. Some animals, especially young ones, have inadequate stress reactions, and they can become exhausted quickly. In this state they are much more susceptible to disease and may develop a severe gastrointestinal infection, pneumonia, distemper or hepatitis. Giving vaccinations the day before shipment will not protect them. It is no real insurance to buy a pup that has been wormed and given its shots. Vaccination procedures must be repeated later under veterinary supervision. Admittedly some stores will guarantee replacement of the pet if it gets sick a few days after you have bought it. Yet few of us would take it back as casually as we would a malfunctioning transistor radio. Within days we are emotionally attached to it, so we seek veterinary advice, and by then it may be too late. The puppy that gave such joy is gone. There is sadness and the children will remember. Perhaps that family will never risk buying a puppy again.

After such a transportation stress, within two weeks after arrival dogs usually develop some infection as a consequence of the stress reaction and increased susceptibility to disease, and a latent or "brewing" infection might flare up within an even shorter time. Many stores do not quarantine their dogs so that they can keep a close eye on them during this recovery period from the stressful experience of transportation. As soon as the shipment arrives, the dogs are put on display and sold.

The prospective buyer should exercise great caution in choosing one of these pups. They may look deceptively healthy and active and have had their shots. Of course, there are exceptions; some large stores may have got the pups from a local breeder, and these pups might have been exposed to no real stress at all. How can one be really sure? The safest possible procedure is to pick up the local newspaper and locate a breeder with pups for sale, then go and see them at the breeder's home.

But whether you buy from pet shop or private breeder, some degree of stress inevitably results when the puppy is adapting to the new environment of the home. Everyone is petting him and he soon gets tired. He needs plenty of sleep and a safe, quiet place as a refuge. Consider the chaos and bustle in the average home at Christmas time—the last place to immerse a young

You go to a dog show like the Westminster to decide on a particular breed. But all of them look great. How do you choose the best?

puppy for the first time! Far better to get the pup a week or so after the Christmas season. Again, one must be on the lookout for poststress infections, which may flare up anytime during the first couple of weeks. So many homes experience sadness over the Christmas period. I once purchased a pup two weeks before Christmas that, in spite of vaccinations, died from distemper encephalitis on Christmas day.

So much for stress, disease and death. The next issue is psychological. Experiments with young dogs have shown that especially at around eight weeks of age pups are extremely sensitive to disturbances, and they tend to remember or to be "marked" psychologically by them for some time, perhaps permanently. A stressful journey to or from the store might cause a more timid individual to react fearfully from then on every time he is put in a shipping crate or in an automobile. Other traumatic experiences that he has had, about which we may never know, may cause him to react fearfully or show a "phobia" to similar things at a later age. He may, for example, appear shy of noises, of suddenly moving objects or of being picked up or handled. Younger pups don't remember quite so well and consequently may be less affected. It is unlikely that they would be shipped at such a young age anyway. Older pups, around twelve to fourteen weeks of age, provided they are well socialized or attached to people, are not innately timid and are much more resilient than they are at eight weeks.

So find out how old the pup is and how long it has been in the store. In a large store, it has probably received very little handling to socialize it to people. Although it has probably seen thousands of people through its glass-fronted cage, it has been touched by very few. It may appear quite normal playing by itself in the cage, but once out of its familiar place it may be shy and withdrawn. It may be incompletely socialized, becoming touch-shy or excessively excited when handled. A resilient puppy would soon snap out of this and would have the built-in abilities to compensate. But a more timid pup might never recover completely, especially after spending a few weeks under conditions of reduced contact with people and with the outside world in general.

Pups need plenty of human contact and experience with all kinds of things during the first few weeks of life, especially between six to twelve weeks of age. If they do not have that contact and experience, they will make very unrewarding and unsatisfying pets—unrewarding because they are harder to train, and unsatisfying because they do not have a close attachment to the master. There are always exceptions, especially in those dogs that are innately outgoing and spunky. But the risk is simply not worth the investment, not only of money, but of effort and emotion.

Pups also need to get out into the world and explore things, and if they have been cooped up in a cage for the first twelve to sixteen weeks of life, they may be very shy of venturing out and facing up to unfamiliar things such as stairs and automobiles. Even though they may be friendly to people, this shyness may never be completely overcome.

I personally would seek out a local breeder and have a good look at the pup's parents or at least at its mother to see what her temperament and looks are like and arrange to take the pup at six to eight weeks of age. Experience in the past and laboratory experiments have shown that this is the best age to get a pup (see later).

The small local pet store might have what I wanted, but even if I knew them to be kind and to take good care of their animals, I would be increasing my risks to some extent in buying a puppy there. These risks would, however, be insignificant compared to the chain pet store and large department store situation, where pups pass from small breeder to wholesaler to retailer, processed like commodities, displayed like luxury items.*

---

*A note for the retailer

Without adequate procedures to ensure that puppies are not psychologically affected by transportation and caging—which may not reveal itself for some weeks—the retailer will be doing his clients severe damage. It cannot be stressed strongly enough that puppies are not commodities. They are developing organisms, extremely susceptible to physical and psychological trauma at around eight weeks of age. They are also extremely dependent on frequent human contact and handling between six to ten weeks of age,

It is pertinent at this point to consider some of the general hazards of shipping both pups and adult dogs, each of which is potentially susceptible to transport trauma, be it a young pup from a breeding kennel going to its new home or a young dog being flown out to his first show. I recently received a dog that had been sent air freight over several hundred miles. A few weeks earlier I had first met him and he was a very fine, tractable dog. But when I took him out of his shipping crate in the basement at home and moved to put a leash on him, he growled, yelped and snapped as my hands moved over his head. I then put the leash down and just tried to stroke him behind the ears as I had done when I first met him. He was thoroughly terrified. Head shy. And it didn't take long to figure out why. His shipping crate was all open two-inch wire mesh—sides, front, back and roof.

Now any animal that is afraid (and this would pretty well include all animals that are being shipped by air) seeks a dark "safe" corner. The place preferred is a crawl hole or at least something with a roof and a hole through which the animal can look out—a den, if you like. Imagine yourself being transported to strange and disturbing places in a glass box. Everyone can see you, the walls of the box prevent you from escaping and the box—double torture—gives you no sense of security. You can be "had" at all angles, from above, from behind, from each side and from in front. This situation would keep you hyperalert for the entire journey, at the end of which you would be poured out of your shipping crate in one blob of jellied nerves.

---

especially if they are kept in separate cages. This handling results in socialization, and without adequate human contact during this six-to-ten-week critical period, they may never develop a close attachment to human beings. If the pups are housed together, they may become too "dog attached." The retailer must also consider the important fact that a pup needs not only human contact but also experience outside its cage—experience in the broadest sense, involving exposure to a variety of inanimate objects which the pup can explore, manipulate, learn about and play with. The small pet store will often employ high school children to come in the late afternoon and take the pups out on the leash or at least play with them and supervise their explorations of the store or stockroom. Of course there are risks of the pups being exposed to infectious diseases if taken outside. Ideally a ten-by-four-foot pen with various play objects should be provided, in which the puppy can be handled and socialized and encouraged to follow the handler around the enclosure. Ten or fifteen minutes of this treatment every other day would be sufficient to protect the pup from any adverse effects of prolonged confinement prior to being sold.

My dog was like this and also completely exhausted after having been hyperalert during such a long journey (even though the luggage compartment of the plane was pressurized and heated). He had been stressed, and such stress can make the animal very susceptible to disease. This psychological exposure stress could lower resistance to any of the infectious viruses, and combined with exposure to cold in the winter, say, as during inevitable delays in shipment, the chances of the dog's developing pneumonia would be increased. Protection with antiserum—globulin—just prior to shipment may help to reduce the chances of an emotionally stressed animal's developing some infection, but it will in no way alleviate the exposure stress per se.

Tranquilizers might be used, but very often, especially on a long journey, the effects of the drug will wear off too soon. And there's nothing worse than a groggy doggy sloshing around in his own mess and mutilating himself inside the crate.

The real problem is the cage. If you have a shipping crate with opaque sides and back, well and good, but if you have a wire one through which the dog can see all around, don't use it except for, say, transporting a confident dog in your own car. If you are going to send a dog by air in one of these exposure cages, first cover the sides and back with some opaque material, either

---

The slight possibility that some pups might not be socialized adequately to other pups as a consequence of social isolation could be eliminated easily by allowing suitable (in terms of size, aggressiveness, etc.) pups to interact freely with each other for four or five minutes every other day. If pet stores were to follow these procedures, the chances of any pup (with the few exceptions of innately shy individuals) being adversely affected by prolonged confinement and inadequate socialization would be eliminated. The retailer should also be aware of the prior treatment of the pups, especially to ensure that during shipment the animals are suitably handled, fed and watered if the journey is long and protected from stresses such as excessive heat, cold, sudden noises, and so on. This is also in his interest, for the pups may later come down with some severe respiratory or gastrointestinal disease after such transportation stress. He should also be sure that the pups are not transported on the same day that they are weaned, for weaning itself can be stressful. Pups should be shipped no sooner than three days after weaning at five or six weeks of age. Even if the pups are not transported any distance, it would be advisable not to accept them until three or more days after they have been completely weaned. They would not only cry excessively as a result of separation from the mother but might also require special handling and coaxing to take solid foods. Weaning is physiologically and emotionally stressful, and to put added stress on the pup by placing it on display for sale would be imprudent.

plywood or heavy-duty canvas. Both you and your dog will be more comfortable with such a cage, because it has now been converted from a show case into a safe refuge. Ventilation holes should be plentiful and on all sides of the cage-crate; baggage might fall or be stacked against the sides of the crate, and the dog could suffocate or develop heat stroke if all sides did not have adequate vents.

The best crate size is an easy question to answer, the rule of thumb being *the smaller the better.* In a large cage a small dog might be thrown about more, while in a cage that just gives him enough room to turn around in, he will fare much better. The sides of the cage will support him and he will not be tossed around as severely.

Many dog owners are not aware of the fact that some airlines have a courier service which can spare the dog considerable trauma. With a courier ticket from the main desk you may carry the crate right to the gate and hand it to the courier, and at the other end of the line the dog can be picked up this way too if you are traveling with him. Airline regulations vary, and this certainly should be looked into.

You might also include some familiar item in the cage such as a rubber bone or blanket. Also get your dog used to the crate a few days prior to shipment by encouraging him to eat and sleep inside, first with the door open and then with it closed.

After sleeping it off for twenty-four hours, my dog seemed much recovered from his ordeal. I just hesitate to think how he might have behaved if he hadn't had such a resilient constitution. Dingos are like that, I guess.

I have discussed some of the factors of purchase and transport which may make a sound-looking little pup quite unsound, susceptible to disease and to behavioral disorders. I have not intentionally slanted the discussion in favor of the private dog breeder and seller over the large department or chain store. The facts and probabilities stand as they are. The prospective pup owner is free to make his own decision.

But do people always know just what they are getting themselves into when they buy a pup? It is a responsibility and commitment that is often overlooked when one sees and purchases a pup on the spur of the moment. There are many things to consider in addition to the question of where to buy. Many people choose a puppy from a good pet store or breeder and still don't realize what they are taking on. They do not understand how much care, attention and training a puppy needs during its early, formative weeks. They may in all innocence neither seek nor be given advice as to what particular breed might best suit their needs in terms of size, temperament and activity requirements. In so many cities the animal shelters fill up with stray dogs and unwanted pups between January and early March. This peak in part reflects the number of Christmas puppies that become too much of a responsibility, too difficult to handle. Why? Partly because of their earlier experiences—psychological traumas and inadequate socialization—before the owners purchased them. And partly because as they begin to grow up they become less and less puppyish and appealing. A cute mongrel pup may grow into an enormous, malproportioned disappointment. Owners may lose interest in their first pup as it matures. They are unconcerned, even relieved if it wanders away to some unknown fate. The more concerned may take it to the animal shelter for humane destruction or possible placement in a foster home. Few of these dogs, though, make good secondhand pets after such an impoverished puppyhood. Like getting a secondhand car, you are never sure until it has been tried out. It might be a good one, but you still wonder why the original owners traded it in!

Clearly, buying a puppy involves some degree of preparation. The prospective owner should be forearmed with a knowledge of the many possible pitfalls. Especially when a pup's earlier life history is either not available or, if known, could possibly have adverse effects on the pup, go and look elsewhere. Dogs are plentiful. Some of the better-run animal shelters keep careful records on the dogs that are being held for a few days before destruction, and you might be lucky and find a good one there. If I had my way, I would like all the dogs in all the animal shelters to have good homes, but so many never make good pets. An experienced person may be able to do well with one of them or with a pup from a dubious or unknown background. This chapter is for the inexperienced, who might be taken in emotionally by an attractive-looking puppy but may lose out both financially and emotionally in the long run.

Having looked at some of the perils of pup buying, we should focus our attention on just what is the best way to get a new pup settled into the house and "at one" with the family. Children should be instructed on how to carry and fondle their new pet and, above all, to respect his needs. A pup needs love and kindness, he needs food and water, he needs exercise and lots of play and he needs privacy, a corner of the room with a basket that is his own. He also needs supervision! Like any human infant, he gets into trouble—recklessly climbing up stairs or onto a sofa and risking a serious fall or chewing and swallowing all sorts of objects, some dangerously hard on the digestion. A puppy also needs appropriate discipline, leash-training, and house-breaking. These common problems will be discussed later.

The new puppy may also have difficulty fitting into the household pack, especially if there is a jealous cat or dog who is already an established member of the family. Giving lots of love and attention to the new puppy will only make it more difficult for him if the other senior animal residents are not given equal time! One should also be on the lookout for a jealous child venting its spleen on the indulged new puppy or, worse still, the pup's becoming the scapegoat for redirected aggression of children frustrated by parental discipline.

Many have said that no family is complete without a dog, and, indeed, I can't recall any Norman Rockwell painting of the American family without a dog somewhere in the picture. Although the dog is a part of our culture, it does not mean that he will automatically become a part of the family. Admittedly there have been thousands of years of selective breeding to

A puppy should be active, playful and assertive, but not too aggressive (top left); He should be well-mannered toward his superiors (top right); He should be inquisitive, uninhibited and not fearful of new things or people (bottom left). All pups are lovable (bottom right), and any one—or all of them—would do! But how do you choose the best and ensure that he will grow up to be a superior dog?

facilitate this, but without careful selection and handling during the first few critical weeks the puppy might not become united with the family and might even prove to be a very unwelcome guest. Careful selection of the proper pup for your life-style is only the first step in ensuring that you will get the best out of your dog and also do what's best for him. The next step, perhaps the most critical one of all, is to ensure that he gets properly socialized. Tender loving care alone will not suffice in making your dog socially well adjusted and emotionally attached to you. In the next chapter we will consider just what underlies play and puppy love.

3

Play and Puppy Love

"PUPPY" IS SYNONYMOUS with "play," but is there a purpose to play? Who would suspect that without love (or affectionate and playful attention) a human baby or puppy could actually die or become an emotional cripple? Is play purely pleasurable or is it perhaps essential for the normal development of any infant mammal? When your pup bounces, bites and wrestles a slipper or clasps it between his forepaws and thrusts to and fro with his pelvis, is he learning, enjoying, or what? The significance of such apparent prey-killing play and sex play and other questions pertaining to play will be explored in this chapter, and the importance of social interaction for the development of social relationships will be shown. The practical significance of this early socialization will be elaborated upon more fully in subsequent chapters.

Puppies may play just for pleasure, for exercise or perhaps for some reason of which we are not yet fully aware. It is generally accepted that play contributes somehow to the development of later behavior, but the picture is far from clear. Much of what is going on is rather automatic—instinctual acts that are "turned on" by the right stimulus. For example, an appropriate object, like a towel or belt, "releases" biting, head-shaking and wrestling. Similarly, a puppy who finds his forelegs clasped around your shoe may play-bite and prey-kill or suddenly behave sexually, much to the embarrassment of a visiting aunt. But there is more to play than this almost reflexlike aspect. There are developmental and evolutionary considerations. Those animals having a long infancy, and therefore spending much time playing, are more intelligent and highly evolved. Children's games become formalized and often imitative of adult roles and transactions (playing house, playing doctors and nurses, etc.). Verbal play is also a significant learning experience for the babbling human infant.

Play seems to expose the young animal—dog or child—to a variety of social situations, so that different social roles, such as being the leader, the follower, the innovator or a cooperative partner are experienced. This leads to improved communication and social flexibility and the individual soon learns of his own limitations and competence in social situations. He therefore becomes socially adjusted. Similarly, play exposes the young animal to a variety of animate and inanimate objects that can be explored, manipulated, and tasted. They may even be used as substitute objects for some more mature object-oriented activity such as prey-killing. The drives to explore and play expose the young animal to the world and this exposure gives him the necessary experience about his environment without which he would be totally incompetent.

The amount of time spent playing tends to decrease as the dog or child gets older. In man it becomes increasingly difficult to separate play from more complex activities engaged in during leisure time. Hobbies such as carpentry and gardening, true sports and games, vicarious involvement of the spectator, and esthetic appreciation derived from listening to music or visiting an art gallery are quite different from any animal form of play. Many formalized adult social interactions, though, such as the stereotyped and ritualized cocktail parties, involve various games, notably play-talking and grooming-talking.

In young animals, play occurs when they have nothing else to do—when they are not afraid or in an unfamiliar place and when they are not cold or hungry. Play may occur at a particular time of day and at a particular place. In many animals, it has virtually disappeared by maturity, although playlike patterns may be seen

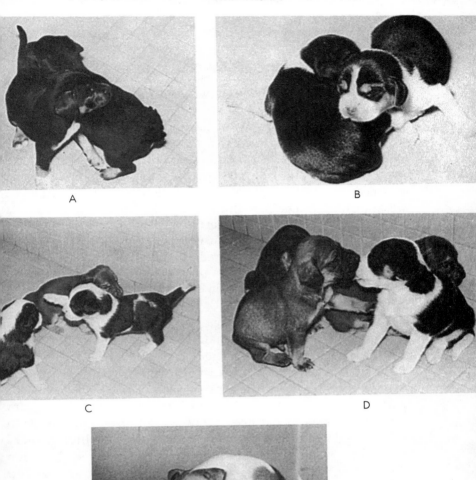

A

B

C

D

E

The earliest play behaviors in pups, long before they develop complex chasing and stalking games, consists of contact circling and learning (a), which may be derived from neonatal contactual circling and "piling" (b). This may be followed by tail or scruff-oriented biting, or by face-oriented pawing (c) and licking (d), or by precocious sex play during courtship and parents will continue to play with their offspring.

Play-soliciting-like behavior has been described in the wolf, fox and coyote, who allegedly perform these movements to lure (or "fascinate") a rabbit toward them. This usually occurs when the rabbit is in fairly open ground and might well become alarmed, run for cover and escape if the predator fox or coyote were to stalk it. The predator reduces the flight distance by its bizarre play-soliciting behavior. As the predator slowly (but playfully!) gets nearer, the inquisitive prey either does not run off or actually approaches the predator to investigate its curious behavior. Some dogs will show this behavior, known as tolling, and good tollers have often been used by sportsmen to lure ducks toward the range of their guns or into concealed net traps.

Various categories of play can be recognized: self-play (tail-chasing, for example), inanimate object play (and exploration, manipulation and even ingestion) and social play with one or more members of the same or of a different species (such as pups playing together or with a cat or owner). A variety of behavior patterns associated with other activities such as prey-killing are seen during play. It has been proposed that group play leads to the young doing things together—cooperative activities. Solitary and inanimate object play in the child is later replaced by group play and even later by team games and sports. In young dogs and wolves, running and chasing things together is the beginning of pack hunting, and such coordinated activities must involve a good deal of communication.

Early learning is important: A hand-raised lamb or beagle will not run with the flock or pack if deprived of experience with its own kind early in life. Play-soliciting patterns may resemble care- or attention-seeking and courtship-soliciting patterns. Sexual behavior such as mounting may occur, or one individual may stalk and leap on the other. Some species, such as fawns and lambs, will run together as though alarmed and chase each other. Badgers play leapfrog, otters may toboggan and young goats may play "king of the castle."

Play-fighting is often seen in most animals during play, differing from actual fighting in that the intensity is lower. Very often, however, during play-fighting an actual fight breaks out. Perhaps one bit the other too hard and the other retaliates defensively. The offender may then learn to bite more gently. Pups develop a "soft" mouth between the third and fourth months of life, but if hand-raised in complete isolation from other pups, they do not acquire this inhibition. When they are first placed together at, say, four months of age, play-chasing and -wrestling soon breaks up when an uninhibited bite is let loose. An inlaw of mine, whom I tend to regard as an outlaw, has a Rhodesian ridgeback that had a very hard mouth by five months of age and was extremely rough when playfully greeting strangers. Apparently, during early puppyhood his misguided master put on thick gloves to roughhouse with him, and consequently he never had any feedback to develop control over his play bites—a situation to be avoided at all costs. When a young pup bites the ungloved hand too hard, which is quite easy to do because milk teeth are like little needles, he should be disciplined immediately, and he will soon acquire good control. If an animal (or child) wants to continue playing with a peer, it soon *learns* to inhibit aggressive or pain-evoking actions. Through this almost sado-masochistic social exploration, individuals learn how far they can go. This may shortly lead to teasing and tantalizing play and, more rarely, sheer sadistic bullying to see the responses of the subordinate. In the dog, fighting between littermates becomes highly ritualized very early in life. The subordinate remains passively submissive and may yelp loudly. Such behavior is said to "cut off" or appease the dominant individual.

Animals and children do have a strong tendency to assert their dominance, and it has been suggested that through play-fighting young animals learn whom they are subordinate to and whom they dominate, without inflicting severe physical injuries on each other. By four months of age, a litter of pups has a relatively stable dominance hierarchy; aggression is now reduced to ritualized displays of domination and subordination, with only occasional outbursts of actual fighting (more frequent in the more aggressive terrier breeds). It is intriguing that while young dogs and wolves engage in long bouts of play at four weeks of age and, as a rule, only later have a fight which determines dominance (some, in fact, never have such a fight), coyotes, in contrast, fight before they play. These cousins of domesticated dogs seem to have to establish dominant-subordinate relationships before they can engage in play and, in contrast to wolves and dogs (which are very close cousins), they seem to require much more social learning before they can control the bite during play-fighting.

Play may, therefore, contribute to the establishment of social relationships based on dominance and subordination and result in the control of aggression within the group. Aggression will be reduced in the group once each member knows its place. When a member is removed from the group or a new individual is introduced, fighting often occurs. This is because the aggression-controlling status hierarchy has been disrupted. It is a good idea, therefore, not to switch pups around in a large kennel from one social group to another, and it is not a good practice to keep pups in separate cages to prevent fighting. If they are housed together from an early age, they will develop a dominance hierarchy without inflicting severe injuries on each other.

When pups get older, it is a sound practice for breeding kennels to house females with females and males with males, so that if a female comes into heat, there will be no males in her enclosure to fight each other as rivals for her favor. Although many breeds of dogs are sociable and playful together as adults, sexual maturity can often cause increased aggression, and in some breeds, such as the terriers, only two or three members of the same sex can be housed together, because a third or fourth might be ganged up on and mutilated or killed. No amount of playful interaction earlier in life seems to prevent this.

It is interesting to note that in some canines, such as the red fox and coyote, the parents become more and more indifferent and even aggressive toward their offspring and eventually leave them, and play-fighting between littermates becomes more and more intense and less inhibited. As a consequence, the litter eventually erupts and disperses. Such a dispersal mechanism is highly adaptive in assuring the spacing out of some species which as adults are solitary hunters, and it contrasts the control of aggression in more social species such as the wolf, where the young stay together and fighting is inhibited through a more ritualized control of aggression and by the establishment of a stable dominance hierarchy or pack order. In the wolf pack, a reversal of dominance may occur during play, when a normally subordinate individual is allowed to dominate a superior member.

Play, the reciprocal interaction between peers or littermates, may not only establish group-coordinated activities but also result in socialization or the development of emotional attachments and preferences. Species preferences and self-identity may also be acquired. For example, a dog raised with a litter of cats prefers the company of strange cats to the company of his own species and shows little interest in or social responsiveness to his own image in a mirror. (We might add that integrated schools might well result in improved socialization in childhood and facilitate subsequent social transactions between different ethnic and social groups.)

Several years ago a friend of mine, Dr. Norman Bleicher, was working as a student assistant in a research laboratory where in one experiment pups had to be weaned early and housed in separate cages. They had no chance to play with each other and were simply cleaned and fed by the caretaker. But they didn't thrive well and many died, death often being attributed to some bacteria that caused pneumonia or enteritis. He was reminded of the work of Dr. René Spitz, who in the early forties described a wasting disease (marasmus) in orphanage infants; this was eliminated and the incidence of disease was reduced while growth rates were increased simply by instructing personnel to fondle and play with the babies. The response was miraculous, and the babies were socially and emotionally far better adjusted when they grew up! Dr. Bleicher instigated a similar regime, giving each pup plenty of human handling and play, play objects in the pen, and an opportunity to play with other pups. The change was just as dramatic as in Spitz's orphanage infants! Puppies, like children, need love and attention and an opportunity to play and interact—otherwise they may die or grow up as socially maladjusted cripples.

And yet independent of play per se, a young animal may develop some kind of an emotional attachment to a loveless caretaker who merely feeds it or to an incubator or surrogate mother that keeps it warm. As Dr. Harry Harlow has shown with his infant rhesus monkeys, the animal becomes pathologically imprinted or attached to such surrogate objects (rather than socialized), and with such early experience its social behavior with its own kind may be severely impaired in later life. The animal appears withdrawn, introverted, asocial, even autistic. Without play, or socialization, its social reactivity is severely restricted. It may react minimally and without overt affect (or affection), and much of its reactivity following social interaction with its own kind, which is stressful, is aggressive or self-directed and extremely bizarre.

Several observers have noted that animals raised in isolation are hyperaggressive, possibly because they have not learned to inhibit aggression during play. They may also be afraid of their own kind because they have never played or become socialized with them. Monkeys raised in isolation make very poor mothers, at least with their first offspring; they apparently show some improvement with later young.

In both dogs and monkeys raised in isolation so that group play and social interaction with peers is denied, sexual behavior is disrupted. The deprived female does not orient and present herself appropriately and the isolation-raised male mounts the female from a variety of ineffectual angles. Possibly intense arousal during the first encounter, a novel situation to say the least for an isolation-raised animal, interferes with the proper orientation for sexual behavior to be consummated. As the male becomes less aroused by the sheer novelty of a receptive female, his sexual behavior becomes more controlled and effective, and vice versa. Indeed, we see much bizarre sexual behavior in

Play in adult dogs is often preceded by social investigation (above), during which the one who is being investigated remains passive. After this, a play-soliciting bow (below) serves to communicate the readiness or mood to play, as does the smiling "play face" expression

normally raised male dogs, who when first put to stud excitedly mount the female and try to copulate with her flank or head. Play would seem to be very important, therefore, for the normal development of social behavior, as witnessed by these experimental animals raised without real mothers or brothers and sisters to interact with.

Is it true, then, that play is important for the later organization of sexual behavior? An animal may learn the body topography of sexual and nonsexual play early in life. Does the play-depriving isolation experiment cause excessive arousal which interferes with effective sexual behavior when partners meet for the first time? These problems, related to novelty and naïveté, are also apparent in normally raised animals (and people), and we cannot be certain to what extent play in early life contributes to the organization of later sexual behavior.* Some animals, notably birds, can become so attached to their caretakers early in life (through imprinting rather than through play) that they show a sexual preference for their caretaker over their own species when they attain sexual maturity. A hand-raised bull moose attempted to mount its keeper when sexually aroused by female moose during the breeding season. He ignored his own females!

It has also been said that play in some way contributes to the later development of hunting, prey-chasing and killing. By playing with each other and with suitable inanimate objects, the young animals learn to perfect a variety of actions which, in the adult, are identifiable with prey-catching and killing. It is more probable that these actions, and those of sexual behavior such as mounting and clasping, are well developed by the time they are first incorporated into play behavior and that little actual learning occurs in play. Coyotes are able to kill their own prey without having played with each other, so that the idea that prey-killing behavior is perfected through play is probably wrong. The

---

*Some group therapists actually teach their patients how to play, and play therapy can be highly effective in improving interpersonal relationships. Is modern man forgetting how to play? Other therapists observe children "acting out" during play sessions and are often able to diagnose various emotional problems that may be troubling the child and that are revealed as the child plays house with mother, father and other figures.

Groups of dogs will run like a pack when they engage in chasing play

act of play may strengthen and speed the execution of these prey-catching actions, but it should be emphasized that these patterns are unlearned or innate.

In children more formalized or structured play may mimic adult activities, such as little children having a mock tea party. Imitative and observational learning occurs in this type of play. The game is very serious, and participants not conforming to the approved sequence are criticized severely by their peers or, if too young, are not included in the game at all. This leads us to the question if actions are essentially innate with regard to prey-catching, how does the lion or wolf cub learn to kill prey much larger and faster than itself? It is most improbable that play activities make any contribution here, and it is more likely that young learn through observation of adults and by participation, at first playing a minor role in chasing and later in attempting to pull down the prey—a parallel to learning by apprenticeship. How the timid wolf cub makes the transition in his first winter to an effective hunter of large game remains to be demonstrated. Apprenticeship, social facilitation and security in numbers, or pack strength, may all have combined influence.

Another interesting fact is that in both dogs and monkeys those that have been hand-raised prefer to play with each other when first introduced rather than with normally raised individuals. Social, and later sexual, preferences may be based on the effects of similar prior experiences or life histories which in some way make animals behave differently to each other. Perhaps young couples are attracted to each other because their compatibility is a result of their having had rather similar experiences earlier in life!

Play behavior in part reflects the pup's temperament, but it is risky just to look at a litter of pups all together and decide which is the best one. Although a puppy is born with a particular temperament substrate which will determine what his personality will be like as an adult, experiences, especially during playful social interaction and the development of relationships

Dogs frequently play with sticks, which seem to serve as "social tools." They may engage in tugs of war, chasing or "parallel play," each with his own stick, or they may chase each other for its possession

during the socialization period, also influence his personality development. In the next chapter, some simple but reliable tests that can be used to evaluate a pup's temperament will be described.

4

How to Evaluate Your Puppy's Temperament

IT WOULD BE a great help to the dog breeder and future owner to be able to quickly evaluate the temperament of puppies. This would not only aid in choosing which has potentially the best show temperament but would also help in deciding what kind of home would best suit the pup. These decisions may seem difficult when the pups are only six to eight weeks of age, but since this is the best time for them to be taken into a new home, some objective knowledge of their temperament would be invaluable. A few expedient and reliable tests can help assess the pup's emerging temperament during the first six weeks of life.

A battery of tests given during these formative weeks could provide a profile of each pup's temperament, and from preliminary studies in my laboratory, the basic temperamental characteristics of young pups are the ones that remain with them throughout life. Those pups rated as outgoing, aggressive, passive or timid and dependent at four or six weeks of age tend to conform to these early ratings when fully mature. What is being observed at this early age is the emerging temperament (or behavioral phenotype), which is the product of the interaction between environment and the innate qualities (or genotype) of the animal. In a litter of pups all raised under more or less the same environmental conditions, the environment will affect pups

55

differently because each one has a different genotype. The
environment can have a "directional effect" on the developing
pup. Thus a basically timid pup may become even more shy and
difficult to handle if raised under very erratic and disturbing
conditions. A basically confident or aggressive pup may become
a submissive urinator if raised by a person who is very dominant
(but not necessarily punishes the pup). Or such a pup raised by
an indulgent owner may become "top dog" in the household and
be an overly confident and aggressive adult.

The breeder can do two things in placing his puppies in the
environment that best fits each one's temperament. He can first
counsel the future owners as to the best way to raise and
discipline a puppy. But this takes time and patience, and all too
often, in spite of painstaking advice, the owners will revert to the
way in which they most enjoy pup raising. Unfortunately, this
may be directly contrary to the pup's temperament. The second
and more expedient thing to do is to match the pup's temperament with the needs and life-style of the future owners. An
active married couple with no children, a retired couple or a
family of boisterous children would each provide different environments suiting some pups better than others. In view of the
fact that in many breeds one particular temperament is most
prevalent, the breeder should advise a quiet retired couple not to
purchase a hyperactive and outgoing terrier or warn a couple
with a vigorous family not to buy one of the more delicate
miniature or toy breeds.

Before describing some basic personality tests, I should point
out that although the general temperament can be clearly
assessed at six weeks, it is not fully mature in the dog until one or
one and a half years. During this maturation phase there are two
major critical or vulnerable periods during which a puppy's
reactions may be drastically altered. The first period is the
socialization period, and if a pup does not get sufficient human
contact during this time (between five and eight weeks) he will
grow up to be people-shy. Or if he has too much human contact
and not enough dog contact or too much human female contact,
he will be respectively shy of dogs and shy of men. A basically

timid pup would be more severely affected and much harder to resocialize successfully at a later age.

The second period is the *period of environmental or place-learning,* which extends from approximately three to five months. If a pup is not taken out much to various and very different places, it will begin to show increasing fear of being in unfamiliar terrain. A pup that has never been out of its pen until three months old will be quite shy outside. More outgoing pups will soon adjust, but innately timid individuals may be permanently institutionalized. As in the socialization period where pups learn about people and begin to show fear of strangers at around eight weeks, so pups also learn about places and some begin to show fear of any changes in the familiar environment, especially between four and five months. The dog may appear sound- or sight-shy, for example. Many grow out of this normal second anxiety period and learn how to handle their fears after discovering that the disturbing stimuli are actually harmless. Other dogs simply do not show this fear period, and because it is clearly evident in all wild canines, it would seem that selective breeding has eliminated this phenomenon in domesticated dogs. But some dogs, perhaps throwbacks to the wild temperament, never seem to cope with their fears. Lois Crisler in her book *Arctic Wild* illustrates this point in her wolves, which apparently took not three months to remain relaxed when she cleaned the dishes but three *years!*

ASSESSMENT OF TEMPERAMENT FROM ONE TO THREE WEEKS

During this period it is useful not only to keep a record of each pup's weight gain but also to make some notes about individual traits which may provide some cues as to subsequent development of temperament. The following behavior may be looked for:

1. Which are the more vigorous pups and which seem less

competitive when nursing? Which win in a fight for a teat and which consistently seem to be outside the "pile"? Which are more often attached to the highly productive posterior or inguinal teats? These may be the litter's more dominant pups.

2. Which of the pups seem to cry more than others, especially when the mother leaves the nest box?

3. Which of the pups are most disturbed and start to cry soonest when placed on a cold surface?

4. Which of the pups squirm and cry when they are handled and which remain quiet and give contentment grunts?

The pups should be observed at weekly intervals and appropriate notes on the above questions taken down. At first it may be difficult to identify each pup, but with careful observation over the first three weeks, their individuality will become increasingly apparent. At first the extremes will be most visible—the most dominant or vigorous, most placid or stable, most hyperactive and most easily distressed pups. Then the more amorphous middle group will shortly begin to differentiate itself.

Although it doesn't sound very nice, the pain test is valuable in determining which pups respond excessively and are hypersensitive and which respond aggressively. The tender web of skin between any of the foretoes is quickly pinched and the pup's reactions noted. In a two- or three-week-old pup, one may note how sustained its distress is after stimulation and how quickly it calms down when petted. Similar notations may be made at six and eight weeks, and also at these later ages one should look out for fear-biting, overt aggression, hysterical, overreactive struggling and escape. Also revealing is how readily the pup will approach and make up after such stimulation.

ASSESSMENT OF TEMPERAMENT FROM
FOUR TO SIX OR EIGHT WEEKS

Because during this period the puppy's nervous system attains relative maturity, a wide battery of tests can be given to evaluate locomotor ability and sensory and emotional reactions to odors, sounds and visual stimuli. Emotional reactions to being separated from mother and littermates, to being placed in a completely unfamiliar place and to being handled by a strange person should also be evaluated. Each pup should be tested separately, because if all are tested together or in pairs a more confident pup may lead out or support a more timid one, the latter therefore appearing almost normal. In the absence of such support, a timid pup, lacking in confidence and dependent on his littermates, would be much easier to identify.

A rating for sociability should also be done, testing each pup's reactions to a person who is first passive, then coaxes the pup to follow, then threatens it and subsequently coaxes it to follow again.

The pups may also be tested together, for there are some useful group tests that can be done. One is competition for food: Which pup is the most aggressive or most subordinate, and when the mother is removed from the pen, which pup comes out first to approach a familiar person, a stranger or a novel object placed in the pen?

Motor Ability

A general rating of each pup's locomotor ability and agility can be scored as follows:

1. Place the pup on a box, from which he has to jump down to the ground—the box is low so that in jumping down he has no chance of injuring himself. Repeat the test several times and see how quickly he gains confidence, for success is reinforcing. Very unsure pups will crouch motionless on top of the box. After a croucher is helped down, how quickly does he learn to get down himself?

2. Place the pup on a slightly higher box, height again appropriate to his size, with a rough-surfaced board down which he can walk. After you have tested to see if he has the insight to get down himself and if he still refuses to descend, how rapidly does he improve after you have gently shown him? Again, with this test a motor ability-confidence score can be made.

3. Using the same setup but varying the angle of the board against the box and its width, more fine-grained tests can be done on older pups to determine their ability to walk down the plank and, conversely, to walk up it to get a food reward placed on top of the box.

4. Also with older pups, say eight to twelve weeks, motor coordination and confidence can be evaluated by leashing the dog and coaxing it to walk along a narrow horizontal plank or two very narrow planks, one for each pair of right and left hind and forelegs.

5. Using a similar box situation, a simple obedience test can be devised. The dog is placed on top of the box and a choke chain is used to inhibit him from attempting to get down. Immediately following the verbal command "stay," the chain is pulled. This test, of course, should be done after tests 1 through 3 and should be repeated on consecutive days, each day the handler moving farther away from the pup but keeping control by voice and a long choke chain. Within a few days it will be easy to evaluate which pups are more obedient, which need more corrections and which can be controlled from a considerable distance.

Sensory and Emotional Tests

1. *Reaction to novel visual and auditory stimuli.* Almost any object that the pups haven't seen or heard before will do for this test. First remove the mother and all pups from the pen, then put inside the cage the novel visual stimulus, say a one-foot-square cardboard box with three-inch-wide black and white stripes on it. Then put the first pup to be tested back in the pen in its nest box (or if there isn't one, put the box at the far end of the pen). Stand to one side so the pup can't see you and record with a stopwatch how long it takes him to approach and investigate the unfamiliar box. After testing all the pups, you might use another visual stimulus, such as a child's wooden or woolly toy.

Again each pup is tested singly in its home cage, an auditory stimulus should be used. You can fix up an electric bell or a can full of pebbles that you pull to and fro with a string. Place the sound-producing equipment under the box that you used in the first test and record as before.

2. *Reaction to isolation.* Which pup is most distressed when it is separated from its mother and littermates, and which are the most stable and confident? This test can be done in two parts. First, remove all animals from their home pen and test each pup alone in his own pen. How soon does he start to cry, if he does at all? Next, test each pup in a completely unfamiliar place where he can't see you and where preferably there are no distracting or diverting stimuli, such as other dogs or interesting objects (furniture, carpets, brooms, etc.) that might interfere. In this test in an unfamiliar place, record how soon a pup starts to show distress. Also note which if any of the pups *explore* the new place. Some will just crouch, shiver and cry, but others will case the joint before crying. The more outgoing pups will show a good deal of exploratory behavior.

Sociability Tests

Each pup is tested alone in his home pen with a familiar person. How readily does the pup approach the handler who is in a squatting position but remaining quite still and silent? Is the pup indifferent, responsive for only a brief time or persistently tail-wagging, face-licking and pawing? When the handler stands up, say after three minutes, does the pup then withdraw, cower or continue to greet him? After two more minutes the silent handler slowly walks around the cage. Does the pup follow readily or does he wander off and do his own thing? After three minutes of testing the pup's following response, the handler turns, faces the pup and calls him, with one hand extended. How fast does the pup respond? Does he cower or greet vigorously? Then the handler shouts loudly and claps his hands for five seconds and backs off, pushing the pup away gently but firmly. He then stands still one or two yards from the pup. How readily does the pup recover from this threat? Is he very timid and does he remain frozen afterward, or is he completely unperturbed? Perhaps a more trainable pup would submissively crouch but recover quickly. The handler finally starts walking around the cage again. How willingly does the pup follow now? Is he more cautious, completely inhibited or apparently unaffected?

A similar sequence of handler reaction tests should be done with each pup in an unfamiliar place. Some insight into fear and dependency might then be gained.

Fear of Strangers

With older pups, say eight to twelve weeks, the same tests should be given by a complete stranger if possible. By this age pups are pretty well socialized and can differentiate strangers from familiar handlers. It will be easy to pick out which pups are more cautious and potentially more likely to be fear-biters or less suited for a particular kind of home.

Emotionality and Problem-Solving Ability

A very simple test consists of setting up an obstacle which the pup has to overcome to reach a person to whom it has been socialized. The obstacle is a six- or eight-foot by four-foot-high barrier of chicken wire through which the pup can see. He is placed behind it, exactly in the middle, and the handler then steps back six feet and calls the pup to come. An unsocialized pup would, of course, be less motivated, but normally raised pups immediately try to approach—directly! They walk right into the barrier, pushing with the nose and crying. They also run up and down and eventually get around the barrier. But to find the end to go around they have to move away from you, as you squat six feet away exactly in the middle of the barrier opposite the point where you first placed the pup. More emotionally disturbed and dependent pups will take much longer to solve the problem. They persist in crying and trying to go through instead of around the obstacle. Next, you can block the left side, and then the right, by placing the barrier against a wall. As the problem gets harder, which pups are the quickest to learn?

It is important in this test not only to rate the pup's performance (how long it takes him to reach you) but also to have some index as to how sociable he is with you. A rather aloof pup who is not very human-attached may solve the problem quickly, because he is less anxious to reach you than the one who is determined to reach you and yet makes a lot of mistakes. The best performance in this test is for a pup to show some distress, almost instantaneous problem-solving ability, and intense greeting when he reaches you. An overemotional pup usually takes a long time to negotiate the barrier, thus clearly demonstrating how excessive emotionality can interfere with learning.

Group Tests

Two group tests can be done to determine which pups are the most aggressive in the litter. An overaggressive female, for example, may not be a willing breeder at some future date. Also, pups that are often very aggressive toward their own kind may be friendly and submissive with people, and it is important therefore to see how a pup relates with his own species.

At feeding time place food in a small but deep bowl and note which pup or pups eat their fill first and keep others away by growling and threatening. This quick test gives an overall view of which are the top and bottom members of the litter. The social rank is usually quite clearly developed by six to eight weeks of age, but changes in rank order can occur at later ages.

The other test is more time-consuming and consists of testing each pup paired with another littermate. Thus, to do a litter of five pups, ten tests will be required, so that each pup is in a round-robin and every possible pair is tested. The test consists of placing the selected pair alone in their home pen and throwing a six-inch piece of fresh beef rib bone into the pen for them to compete for. The most possessive is the winner, although in some pairs there may be no competition as both lie together and chew opposite ends of the bone. In such cases, their dominance status is probably equal. All pups should be hungry before the test, and with large litters tests should be spaced out over a few days. This is because defeat or success in competition may influence subsequent tests, as when a recent winner is pitted against a recent loser.

HANDLER TESTS

Leash tests. The behavior of pups wearing a collar or harness as they are trained to follow on the leash is worth noting. Which struggle and fight or refuse to follow, and which learn fastest to obey simple leash commands? With older pups, their readiness to follow on a leash through a dark, narrow doorway, past and around some frightening novel object (such as a rattling grocery cart), up and down a flight of stairs, under a low overhang, down a sudden one- or two-foot curb, through a puddle of water, over different textures, gravel, grass, aluminum foil or noisy wrapping paper, etc., can give valuable information as to the pup's temperament. Is he headstrong, clumsy and inattentive, cautious and observant, or timid and unreliable? These leash tests have been used to evaluate pups as future guide dogs for the blind and have been found very reliable in giving a good and objective measure of the pup's potentials.

"Competitive spirit" test. An effective test to assess which pups are more spirited and potentially more suitable for aggression-training is to set up an aggressive-play situation between handler and pup. A two-foot-long strip of canvas is wiggled on the ground and the pup enticed to seize it. A tug of war is then initiated. The latency of response and general vigor of the pup can be rated on a simple numerical basis (0 = no response, 1 = weak response—pup soon loses interest and only nibbles the teaser, 2 = moderate response—pup bites and pulls, 3 = strong response—pup bites, pulls, growls, shakes head violently, etc.).

Does the pup cease to pull when the handler shouts and beats the ground with one hand? Is the pup now aggressive and virtually out of control (and therefore possibly not the best one for training)? Does the pup stop but resume the game when the handler stops shouting and instead encourages the pup, or is the pup now completely inhibited and afraid?

The final part of this test is to let the pup win. The handler lets go of the teaser and records whether the pup then stops playing and waits for him to participate or instead runs off "prey-killing" the play object. If this latter normal reaction occurs, does the pup readily surrender the teaser when the handler tries to get it, or is he overly possessive and difficult to communicate with?

TESTS FOR HUNTING DOGS

For hunting dogs many people have devised their own tests to determine which pup in the litter is potentially the best bet for training. The earlier basic tests described above are very relevant here, because they give a good profile of the pup's emotionality and sociability. Specialist tests in the absence of such basic tests are of little value. Some people will, for example, throw a dead pheasant or quail into a litter of pointers and choose the one that gets it first. Other people, just looking for a pet, will choose the pup that comes up to the front of the cage first. In both instances the owners might be choosing the most aggressive dog and not necessarily the most trainable or most human-oriented individual. Pups will compete for the pheasant as they will compete for first place by the cage front, and the most dominant one wins. And he is the one chosen—a bad choice very often.

Suitable "specialist" tests:

1. Place a caged live quail or rabbit in the pen and determine which pups show the greatest interest and which persevere most in investigating and trying to get into the cage. Which pups point, which crouch, which withdraw and show fear, which are excessively vocal? Again, it is of value first to test each pup alone with the caged stimulus and then test the whole litter together.

2. With a long string attached to a rabbit skin or bird feathers, the readiness of some breeds to chase, with or without giving voice, can be evaluated. When a pup is allowed to seize the stimulus, does he give it up readily, has he a soft mouth, does he

guard it or does he rip it up instantly? Does he respond to voice by appropriately retrieving, does he immediately stop destroying it or does he try to make off with his prize?

3. With the same object on a string, does the pup balk at going through a puddle or shallow pond? Is he water-shy?

4. Pups aged eight to twelve weeks are not too young for preliminary tests of their trailing or tracking abilities. The first requirement is that they should be highly excited by a novel odor and should readily follow a simple trail which has been dragged using any of the commercially available or naturally derived animal odors (deer musk, etc.). As in all earlier tests, pups should first be tested singly, because less motivated and more timid pups may be supported or socially facilitated by more outgoing littermates if tested in a group.

5. Gun-shyness and fear of being in the field—that is, in an unfamiliar place—are common problems in young gun dogs. Some get this way because an overzealous owner pushes them too fast. Others are basically more timid—shy of sudden noises or of being in an unfamiliar place. The tendency to develop these and other problems can be tested for in sporting dog puppies not by devising new specialist tests but by using the basic tests outlined earlier in this chapter.

Certain traits and temperamental nuances are often inherited, but to determine such, one must know something about the behavior of the parents and of their offspring and, if possible, of the progeny of the dog in question. A specific phobia such as gun-shyness is obviously not inherited per se, but the susceptibility to develop such a specific sound-shyness might indeed be inherited.

The inheritance of behavior and temperament is complex, for the characteristics of a breed comprise a combination of several independently inherited traits which are modified by genetic factors. No trait is inherited as such; genetic factors are transmitted by inheritance, but the traits themselves are modified by interacting genetic and environmental factors. Training and early experience greatly influence these traits, and it is the selection of traits which facilitate easier training to perform particular tasks that differentiates one breed from another and individuals within the breed.

The most widespread use of modern dogs is for companionship, and a great variety, differing widely in size and shape, have been produced. A physically small, easily dominated and controlled dog is the most popular type, showing expressive affection-seeking behavior toward the owner and a mild degree of territorial defensive behavior in that it will bark when strangers are near.

There is a wide series of dogs that covers the whole spectrum of behavior, each breed having certain selected characteristics that enable it to perform maximally a certain behavior pattern, such as scent-trailing and pack coordination in hounds, while other behavior traits are reduced, such as aggression and fighting in hounds.

Breed variations in aggressive behavior, emotionality and conditionability have been found. Some dogs, such as beagles, can be housed in large numbers, for they are nonaggressive; other more aggressive breeds are better kept in pairs or threes, because the establishment of a hierarchical society involves much fighting which many continue if the social order is unstable or the subordinate of the group is constantly victimized. In mixed groups of dogs it has been found that one particular breed is consistently dominant, so it is possible that dominance in genetically heterogenous groups is determined by heredity.

Several researchers have reported that defensive behavior is inherited, and also fear of noise (sound-shyness) and touch (touch-shyness) may be inherited. There are breed differences in pain sensitivity, terriers notably being very resistant.

The herding and droving behavior of sheep dogs appears early in life during play and is stronger and more compulsive in those pups who will be excellent adult working dogs. The early emergence of such traits, such as herding in sheep dogs and pointing in gun dogs facilitates the selection of desirable pups from the litter who strongly manifest these activities. Experience has shown that these dogs who have an innate response which can be brought out or reinforced further by training are superior to their littermates.

We have a great variety of dogs who differ in many ways from their wolf ancestors and have developed behavior patterns not seen in the wolf. Inheritance of certain traits has a strong influence on later behavior, but it is the interaction of inherited (genetic) and environmental factors, especially early in life during the critical period of socialization, that determines the behavior of the mature animal. Training to perform particular tasks has been facilitated by selecting desirable traits which are inherited, and the best results can be obtained by adopting standard training procedures. "Training" in this case is in effect the environment, which interacts with the temperament or inherited constitution of the animal. It must be remembered that constitution may be altered by poor selective breeding, and consequently much compensatory training will be required. We must also be aware of the fact that training procedures for one type of dog may be ineffectual for another breed. Mild punishment is effective in inhibiting undesirable activities in beagles, for example, but punishing a terrier may cause resistance, for these dogs are aggressive and associate pain with fighting. Reward training is effective for most dogs, and food or handling are good reinforcers. Or the activity alone may be rewarding in itself; tracking dogs, for example, get considerable reward simply by performing their chosen task.

In complicated training procedures it is advisable to progress slowly, step by step, for overstimulation may cause confusion and inhibition of earlier learned responses; fixations or maladaptive responses may result and become habits which are difficult to eradicate. Forced training using a leash and choke chain is popular among obedience schools; a command which acts as a conditioning stimulus followed by a tug on the leash is a simple conditioning procedure to train dogs to respond to command of voice. The leash can later be discarded once the conditioned response is established. Food reward may be used similarly. It must be remembered that training does not produce a new pattern of behavior but rather it establishes control over the emergence of these patterns. Underlying the gradual development of the pup's temperament and behavior are a number of intriguing changes in the structure and function of the brain. The changes that are taking place in the brain during the first few weeks are indirectly reflected in the puppy's behavior. These changes will be described in the following chapter and will be tied in with the pup's overt behavior and emotional reactions.

5

How Your Dog's Brain and
Behavior Develop

ONE OF THE fascinating things about being around young animals, and especially puppies and children, is to have the opportunity to observe how they develop, how they begin to explore the world, to manipulate objects and interact with each other. In the two previous chapters I have described some of the subtle patterns of behavior development that pups go through during their early formative weeks. Such knowledge not only helps us to deeply appreciate some of the wonderful phenomena of life and of development, it also gives greater insight into things around us and into the way in which evolution is reflected in an animal's development as he adapts to his particular world. So many people own young pets and potentially they provide a great source of learning material, especially for children.

In this chapter I want to describe some of the major events that are occurring in the pup's brain during the first few weeks of life from the structural and functional view. The development of various behaviors up to full maturity will also be followed. Many people regard the brain as a "black box" and they prefer to speculate about psychological issues such as ego development, personality and emotionality without having to consider how the brain is really functioning. Others react against this approach and try to investigate what's going on inside the black box. They look at the structure of the brain under high-powered microscopes and place electrodes in various regions to record activity while the subject is doing such things as listening, learning or engaging in social interaction with another animal. The next step to explore the secrets inside the black box is to stimulate certain areas of the brain with very weak electrical currents or with chemicals. If, for example, one part of the brain of a cat, the hypothalamus, is stimulated, a ragelike reaction occurs, causing the subject to behave as though it were defending itself from an adversary. If the lateral nucleus of the hypothalamus of a rat is stimulated, the animal will eat voraciously. On the other hand, if this region is destroyed with a strong electrical current causing the nerve cells to coagulate, the rat stops eating altogether. We can therefore say that this region is an important center for controlling feeding behavior. Recently some researchers have put electrodes in various parts of a rat's brain and found that the rat will actually work, pressing a bar, in order to receive a small amount of electrical stimulation. Electrodes in such regions may be in "pleasure" centers of the brain. On the other hand, a rat will press a bar to stop electrical stimulation through electrodes placed in other regions of the brain—presumably in pain or discomfort centers.

Several researchers have found that if they stimulate one aggregation of nerves in a region of the forebrain known as the amygdala, extremely aggressive reactions may be turned on. People with tumors in this region may be hyperaggressive or hypersexual. But if this region is destroyed, aggressive reactions may be abolished. A wild sewer rat can be made tame after its amygdalae have been destroyed.

It is through these studies and careful follow-ups of brain disorders in man that we are beginning to understand some of the subtleties of brain function. Although several apparently specific centers controlling behavior such as sex, aggression and eating have been identified, one is struck by the fact that the brain is a highly complex and integrated structure which is capable of remarkable compensation when some of these so-called specific centers are destroyed. It is through detailed studies of the developing brain that we can really begin to understand how different centers develop and how the brain becomes an integrated system.

The patterning of development of various centers is under genetic control. This control, which has evolved over thousands of years, is such that the animal is equipped to perceive, respond and otherwise adapt to essentially anticipated environmental conditions and circumstances. Thus at birth the pup is endowed with already well-formed sensors which enable it to locate a nipple, and it can suck. This is a beautiful example of an unlearned, genetically programmed behavior—of an instinct or innate predisposition and ability. Some improvement in locating the nipple and in the strength and efficiency of sucking does occur, indicating that this improvement is due to experience or learning—often a very simple kind of conditioning. Pups have the ability to learn or become conditioned to odors, such as aniseed oil, at as early an age as one day.

Another process which results in improvement in some behavior patterns is simply maturation—the increasing functional efficiency of moving parts, such as the limbs or muscles coordinating sucking and swallowing, and the improved sensing and discriminating abilities of the sense organs of touch, taste, smell, balance, equilibrium and, later, sight and hearing. Another beautiful example of the brain's "anticipating" what the environment is going to provide is to be found in the human brain at birth. A well-developed speech center, known as Broca's area, is present, and its development during fetal life is genetically programmed. Clearly, therefore, the brain is not a "blank slate" or *tabula rasa* at birth; it comes with certain abilities and expectancies already "wired in."

When we look at the structure of the brain and its function in young animals that have not yet had any experiences that could have influenced the brain, we see that the environmentalist's argument is unfounded. But the other argument that everything is preformed or innate and simply needs the appropriate trigger to switch on the behavior is equally untenable. What we find, in fact, is that there is an innate or genetically programmed neural substrate, or blueprint, of the brain centers already laid out, the action and interaction of which is determined by varying degrees of experience. Some actions, such as sucking, require very little experience, for they are turned on or released like reflexes by appropriate stimulation. Other often more complex actions require a good deal of experience and are less under predominantly instinctual control. Konrad Lorenz uses the term instinct-training conditioning, where an innate, or instinctual, predisposition to respond is reinforced or shaped by experience. Following a trail and discriminating it from others and the ability to efficiently catch, kill and dissect prey are good examples. The innate predisposition to follow odor trails and small moving objects is seen in all pups as they explore and play. Their activities then expose them to appropriate experiences from which they benefit by improving their abilities to track and hunt.

Two other points of general interest about the developing brain should be mentioned before we deal with some specific aspects of brain development in the dog. If the adult brain is deprived of oxygen for five to ten minutes, permanent damage and even death may follow. But a newborn pup's brain is far more resistant, and some colleagues in Czechoslovakia have found that a newborn pup is three times more resistant than an adult, while a four-week-old pup is just as susceptible as an adult. This is because the newborn pup's brain can continue its metabolism for some time even when the oxygen supply is zero. It is able to break down proteins and continue to function, while the adult brain can only utilize carbohydrates, for which it requires a good deal of oxygen. This means that the pup at birth is protected to some degree against the deleterious effects of a protracted birth, which might otherwise, as a consequence of lack of oxygen (hypoxia), cause brain damage.

The second intriguing thing about the developing, or un-developed, brain is its incredible ability to reorganize and compensate for damage to certain regions. If the visual cortex—that part of the forebrain that enables us to consciously perceive what is before the eyes—is removed in an adult cat, for example, it is virtually blind. But if the same region is removed in a newborn kitten, it will be able to see very well as an adult. Many such experiments have shown how remarkably well the

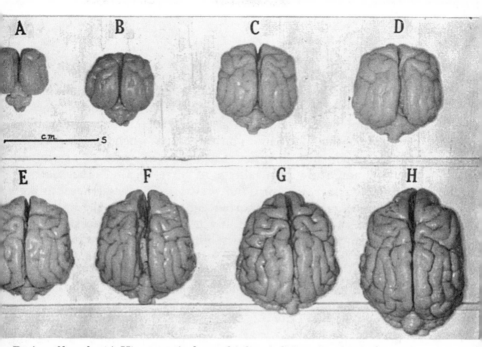

Brains of beagles (A-H), respectively aged 1 day, 1, 2, 3, 4, 6 and 8 weeks, and adult. The grooves and ridges (sulci and gyri) do not attain adultlike patterning until 3 weeks. The brain then continues to increase in size, especially lengthwise as the frontal lobes of the forebrain (F) grow out

developing brain can reorganize and compensate for quite extensive damage. Some recent studies have shown that if a young rat or dog is superstimulated during the early period of development, its brain matures faster and may be larger than normal, containing more and often larger nerve cells that have longer and more elaborate connecting processes. The environment can therefore have an effect on brain structure. Doing the opposite—depriving an animal of experiences by raising it in isolation—has the opposite effect: The brain is smaller and nerve cells are smaller, fewer in number and with less connecting processes than normal.

At birth the pup's brain is only partly developed. Centers in the more posterior parts of the brain, the brainstem, that regulate the heartbeat, breathing and balance or equilibrium are quite well developed at this time. Temperature regulation and associated body metabolism, which are also controlled by the brain, are poorly developed. The newborn pup is to some extent like a reptile, for as the surrounding temperature falls, so does its body temperature. Between two and three weeks the centers controlling these functions mature, so that when the temperature falls, the pup now burns more calories in order to prevent its body temperature from falling. At birth we find other parts of the nervous system are quite mature. The facial nerve is well developed, and this is important since it enables the pup to use its head as a sensor or probe: It will avoid cold surfaces and move toward soft, warm ones. This ability would seem to match with the pup's need to be able to locate the nipple for food and to find warmth by contact and so regulate its body temperature behaviorally, rather than metabolically, by crawling away from very hot and very cold areas.

When we look at the spinal cord at birth, we find that the nerve tracts carrying information to the brain about what's going on in other parts of the body, such as touch, temperature and pain sensations, are well formed. These tracts go into the brain but at birth they have not grown very far. This means that the pup is sensitive to pain, for example, but only in a very diffuse, semireflexive kind of way. It is only later when the nerve connections link up with the forebrain that the pup really begins to localize and consciously perceive pain.

Dr. Jack Werboff, a colleague and friend, while at Jackson Laboratory in Bar Harbor, Maine, found that pups during the first few days of life can actually learn to discriminate between skin sensations differing in texture. He found that a pup will make a choice of crawling on a soft rather than a rough surface if he is rewarded after a few seconds' crawling by finding a bottle of formula. And the opposite is true: A pup can be trained to choose the rough rather than the soft surface in a simple Y maze if at the end of the rough run he is rewarded. Clearly the pup during its first few days of life does have considerable learning ability, and a close look at the nervous system helps us to understand how this is possible. The fact that the olfactory or smell-sensing system is surprisingly mature at birth corroborates my findings that if pups are exposed to aniseed oil placed around

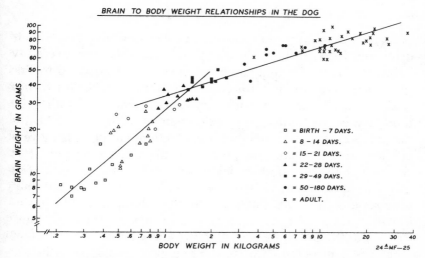

BRAIN TO BODY WEIGHT RELATIONSHIPS IN THE DOG

□ = BIRTH – 7 DAYS.
△ = 8 – 14 DAYS.
○ = 15 – 21 DAYS.
▲ = 22 – 28 DAYS.
■ = 29 – 49 DAYS.
● = 50 – 180 DAYS.
x = ADULT.

BRAIN WEIGHT IN GRAMS

BODY WEIGHT IN KILOGRAMS

24△MF—25

Graph showing how rapidly the dog's brain grows in relation to the body up to 5 to 6 weeks of age, after which time brain growth is more gradual

the nipples of their mother, they will crawl behind a Q-tip soaked in aniseed oil twenty-four hours later if they are cold or hungry. Pups that have never had this prior exposure withdraw quite violently when a Q-tip is placed anywhere near their noses.

A close look at the nerves that pass down the spinal cord to regulate movements of the limbs reveals that many are very well developed at birth, more so in connection with the forelimbs than with the hind. This difference ties in with the newborn pup's coordinated use of the forelimbs for crawling and nursing, while the hind limbs are poorly coordinated and are for the most part simply dragged around. Most of these nerves connect up with only the lower reflex centers of the brain, so that actions such as crawling and withdrawing a foot if it is pinched are essentially involuntary or reflexive. Nerve pathways for voluntary movements, for refined, consciously coordinated actions, which originate in the forebrain, develop much later, between three and four weeks of age.

Many of you have seen a mother lick her pups and lap up their urine and feces. In fact, she completely controls their excretory behavior during the first three weeks or so, for pups up to this time have, like human babies, no voluntary control. But if they were messing the nest with constant evacuations while the mother was out hunting, it would soon be filthy and a health hazard. So nature, through natural selection, has provided a very efficient solution, for the pup will only evacuate when it is stimulated by the mother licking its anus and genitals. The response is a simple, involuntary reflex. Later, as the pup matures and can consciously control these functions, it begins to evacuate in a particular place some distance from the den. When we look at the brain, we find that the nerve tracts in the frontal lobes that control these functions are poorly developed until four to five weeks, which ties in well with what we see behaviorally.

The frontal lobes are also associated with memory and learning, and young pups begin to learn a great deal once these lobes or association areas reach a sufficient degree of maturity around five to six weeks. A week or so prior to this, other parts of the forebrain mature (between three and four weeks). The first to show signs of maturity are the forebrain regions concerned with voluntary control of movements and conscious perception and localization of body stimulation—of touch, stroking, and so on. Shortly after, the centers concerned with conscious perception of visual and auditory sensations are maturing. By four weeks of age, therefore, much of the pup's brain has matured, but it is not until between five and six weeks that the brain becomes an "integrated" system.

One of the best indications that we have of the developmental changes taking place in the dog comes from the electro-encephalograph (EEG), or brain wave studies. These are picked up from various parts of the brain, and after being magnified as waves of activity, or electrical potentials, they are drawn by fine pens on an ink-recording machine. The electrical activity of the pup's brain is very weak during the first two weeks, the electrical potentials being few and very low in amplitude. Between three and four weeks there is a marked increase in

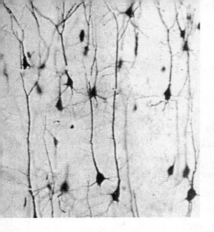

High-power photograph of neurons from the motor region of the dog's cerebrum at 10 weeks of age. Note how the neurons are arranged in rows or layers

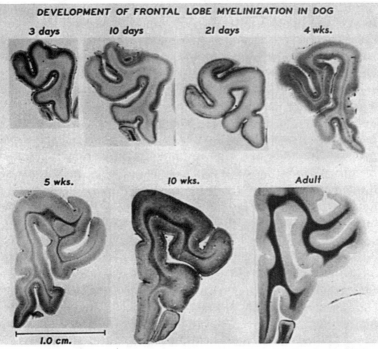

DEVELOPMENT OF FRONTAL LOBE MYELINIZATION IN DOG

3 days   10 days   21 days   4 wks.

5 wks.   10 wks.   Adult

1.0 cm.

Development of myelin (M) in the frontal lobe of the dog forebrain. Myelin is a fatty substance around nerve fibers associated with nerve transmission, and increasing quantities of myelin are related to increasing levels of functional activity. The first traces of myelin in this part of the dog's brain are seen at 4 weeks, at which time the pup rapidly develops socioemotional reactions and elaborates increasingly complex learning abilities strength, which reaches more or less the adult level between four and five weeks.

One part of the hind region of the brain, which is known as the reticular formation and which actually keeps the brain awake or alert, is poorly developed at birth. This is why pups spend so much time sleeping, and it is not until after four weeks of age that they can maintain wakefulness for any appreciable length of time. So much of their sleep early in life is of the "activated" kind; they lie quivering and twitching for long periods. The duration of this activated sleep decreases over the first three weeks, and in older animals (and people) this represents the deep dreaming stage of sleep. The center for this type of sleep is in the base of the brain, and it develops before a second sleep center, which begins to function at around three weeks. This other center switches off the forebrain and gives rise to quiet sleep: The animal (or person) just lies very relaxed and yet is quite easy to awaken and is not disoriented. It is much harder to wake up from the deeper dreaming state, and a short period of disorientation occurs.

Our trip into the black box has, I hope, provided some insight into how the brain develops and how its development can be tied in with what behavior the pup is capable of at various ages. Having looked at how the brain of the dog develops, we will now consider some more general aspects of the development of the entire behavior repertoire from birth through to maturity.

The puppy develops through four clearly recognizable stages, each one being characterized by certain behavior patterns and emotional reactions. The first is the neonatal stage, during which the immature puppy remains in its nest (weeks one and two). This is followed by the transition period, during which time the pup's abilities to walk, hear and see are rapidly maturing (week three). A period of socialization (from weeks four to twelve) follows, and from about three months onward the juvenile period persists until full sexual maturity.

A drawing made from a highly magnified portion of an adult dog's forebrain showing some of the elaborate and beautiful cells. Some can be identified as impulse-generating and -transmitting nerve cells (f); others provide support and nutriment for the nerve cells and are called glia, of which there are many different kinds (a, b, c, d, e, g and h). Some have connections with blood vessels (BV) and provide a link between the circulation and nerve cells which they may nurture

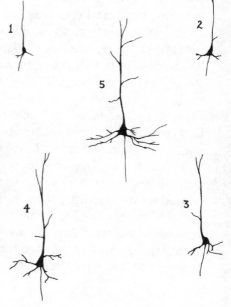

Diagram of how a nerve cell or neuron develops in the dog's forebrain at 1 day, 1, 2, 4 and 6 weeks respectively. Note how the branching processes grow out from the nerve cell and become increasingly elaborate. The more processes there are, the more connections can be linked up with other nerve cells from distant regions of the brain

NEONATAL AND TRANSITIONAL PERIODS

The pup is frequently delivered within its fetal membranes. The bitch licks these off and ingests them and also severs the umbilical cord with the carnassial, or large molar, teeth. Her attention is not focused exclusively on the pup at this time, for she also licks her vulva and any fetal fluids that are on the ground. As the pup is stimulated by the tongue of the bitch during removal of the membranes, it responds violently by squirming from side to side and eventually cries when spontaneous breathing is established and excess fluids escape from the upper respiratory tract.

Before this initial stimulation, the pup lies with little or no spontaneous movement within the intact fetal membranes. The licking and nosing stimulation by the mother subsequently evokes a "mass response," and the pup squirms, rights itself, crawls (rooting reflex) and, after a short period of irregular gasping respiration, commences to breathe regularly and to vocalize (mewing). The severed umbilical cord continues to bleed for some time, and this area is licked intensively by the mother. Such contact reflexively stimulates the pup to breathe. Other parts of the body are licked also. When the face and top of the head are stimulated, the pup crawls forward. Mere contact with the leg of the mother will also stimulate this rooting and eventually the pup locates the teats. When the pup is removed from the nest and is placed on a cold surface, distress calling, pivoting and rooting head movements are seen; this behavior ceases upon contact with a warm, soft object.

Through the first two to three weeks, the bitch stimulates urination by licking and also eats up all urine and feces that are passed by the pups. By three to three and a half weeks the pups are able to stand and to follow the mother. They show the rooting response and reach up to the teats of the bitch while she is standing up. Pups at this age remain quite still while the bitch is licking the anogenital region.

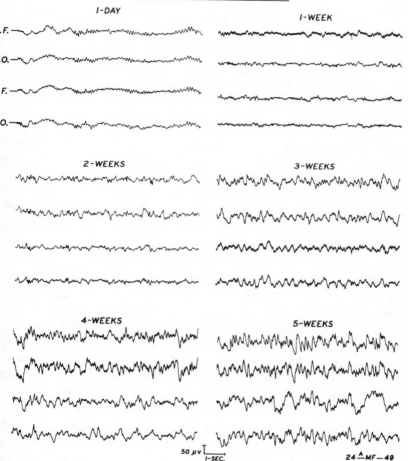

Brain wave (EEG) records of pups at various ages, showing that there is an increase in activity, in the amplitude or height of the brain waves and in the number of waves as the animal gets older. Relatively mature activity emerges between 4 to 5 weeks of age

SOCIALIZATION PERIOD

Occasionally, the bitch will regurgitate food for the litter from four to five weeks onward. This is not uncommon in the domesticated dog and is triggered partly by the mere presence of the pups and partly by the pups' licking the face and mouth of the bitch.

Before four to five weeks of age, the pups sleep in a "pile" when the mother is out of the nest, undoubtedly a heat-conservation mechanism. When two or three pups are placed together on a cold surface, they crawl around and over each other (contactual circling). After three weeks of age, regulation of body temperature is well developed, and the pups tend to sleep in a row instead of a heap, unless the whelping quarters are excessively cold.

From three and a half to four weeks of age the pups begin to interact playfully, chewing each other's ears and licking and pawing at each other's faces. From this age the pups learn, possibly through play, how much pain they can inflict on each other as a result of chewing and biting. These early rudimentary play responses become more variable as visual and locomotor abilities improve. Playful fighting, chasing, scruff holding and prey-killing head-shaking movements appear between four and five weeks, together with pouncing, snapping and aggressive vocalization, such as growling and snarling with the teeth bared. Submissive postures and care- and play-soliciting gestures appear too, including rolling over onto one side, hindleg raising and whining (as distinct from "distress" calling) and licking and foreleg raising.

The facial expressiveness of the pup at five weeks contrasts with the masklike appearance of three-week-old pups. This is due especially to the development of expressive ear movements, elongation of the muzzle and possibly to improved functioning of the muscles controlling elevation of the lips and display of the teeth. Also the repertoire of vocal patterns improves during this period from three to five weeks.

At four to five weeks of age, pups frequently carry small

As in the wolf, the pups may "mob" the mother, who in turn regurgitates food for them

After ejaculation the sire and bitch become tied or locked together. This is accompanied by much excitement and investigation by other dogs. A female may mount and show male sexual activities, including clasping and thrusting. This may be a sign of aggressive domination, but such behavior is also symptomatic of cystic ovaries or other hormonal disturbances in masculinized or nymphomanic dogs

objects in their mouths and engage in tugs-of-war. Soon afterward a defensive-protective pattern emerges in which the pup vigorously guards (prey-guarding?) a particular object or morsel of food. Several pups may follow one littermate who is carrying something in its mouth. These are the first signs of coordinated group activity. A sudden disturbing noise will frequently cause the entire litter to withdraw rapidly. Again, this is a coordinated group, or allelomimetic, response. It is at this age that pups begin to defecate and urinate in one particular area of their living quarters, usually some distance from the nest.

By six weeks of age, most of the species-characteristic behavior patterns are present, notably the face-licking greeting response, inguinal or groin approach, inguinal presentation and anal and genital investigation. Although the mature male hindleg-raising urination pattern does not develop until around puberty, fragments of sexual behavior, such as mounting, clasping and pelvic thrusts are seen during play as early as six weeks, predominantly in male pups.

JUVENILE PERIOD

What might be called an environmental, or situational, fear emerges around four to five months of age. The dog reacts fearfully when in an unfamiliar place or when its familiar environment is in some way altered. There may be later periods of emotional instability, but these remain to be identified. According to Russian workers, the temperament of the dog does not reach stabilized maturity until one to one and a half years of age, and possibly even later in slow-maturing breeds. It would seem that if pups experience something extremely unpleasant during one of these sensitive fear periods, they may be permanently traumatized or require a good deal of gentle handling and desensitizing in order to overcome their phobias.

It is beyond the scope of this book to go into an in-depth account of adult canine behavior patterns. Instead, a general

Bitch showing normal maternal reactions, removing fetal membranes from newborn pup, which are eaten. Then the umbilical cord is severed and the pup is thoroughly licked dry and soon after finds a teat and begins to nurse. Some bitches will not allow pups to nurse until all have been born. Maternal behavior improves with experience and is not entirely instinctive overview will be presented with emphasis on some of the more interesting highlights of canine social behavior.

ADULT BEHAVIOR

The Senses

Dogs have remarkable olfactory (smell) abilities, and this in part may be attributed to their vomeronasal organ, a second smell organ situated in the roof of the mouth behind the front teeth. It is absent in man. Dogs are able to track and locate specific objects or individuals, and these accomplishments are indicative of two separate abilities: great olfactory acuity, permitting them to detect minute traces of odor, and the ability to discriminate between very similar odors, as, for example, between twins. Some scientists claim that the dog's olfactory sensitivity is from 1 to 100,000,000 times greater than man's, but this may not be true. The olfactory receptor area of the brain is much greater in dog than in man and there are indications based on this that show that the dog has a far superior olfactory acuity, although *individual* olfactory cells may have very similar sensitivity in both dog and man. The dog simply has more of them.

The dog also has extremely well-developed auditory abilities. Below frequencies of 250 cycles per second, man and dog have relatively similar acuity, but above this, the dog's is far greater. The dog can detect high frequencies that the human ear cannot—hence the silent dog whistle.

Visual abilities vary from one breed of dog to another. They can discriminate between different light intensities almost as well as man, but their form and pattern discrimination is inferior. They are also color-blind.

Behavior Patterns

The need for exercise varies from one breed to another, some having a low activity requirement, while others have a high one. In confinement the latter may develop stereotyped pacing and weaving patterns which may help to satisfy the high activity drive. This is an important consideration when choosing a dog that, for example, is to be kept in a small apartment. Most working dogs and terriers possessing a high activity drive will need some outdoor exercise and if confined may develop destructive tendencies in the household or by virtue of their sustained hyperactivity become very irritating companions.

Ingestive Behavior

One of the most significant points about ingestive behavior is that of social facilitation. Dogs, and especially pups, will eat more when fed in groups than if fed singly. A satiated puppy that has been fed alone will gorge itself with more food if another pup is put with it. Fighting more frequently occurs at feeding time, and dogs low in the hierarchy may not receive sufficient food while the "top dog" gorges itself. To avoid this, it is a good idea to provide ad-lib dry food via a feed hopper (provided none of the dogs are overeaters) or to feed the dogs out of not one but several food bowls, so that competition over a single and limited source of food is eliminated. Emotional factors especially influence eating, notably depression, separation anxiety and fear. Occasionally dogs will overeat in order to relieve anxiety, but such cases are rare. Some examples of emotional disturbances that influence ingestive behavior will be given in Chapter 12.

Coprophagia (eating feces) is a common vice in dogs. In caged or otherwise confined dogs it may be attributable to boredom, and the provision of play objects such as a ball or a length of garden hose may be sufficient to break this habit. Nutritionists have claimed that a little raw liver in the diet may stop some dogs from coprophagia, and this is certainly worth trying. Dogs will also eat all kinds of objects, especially when they are young. This is part of normal exploratory oral and ingestive behavior, and one should be on the lookout for any objects that might splinter and perforate or block the pup's alimentary tract. Provide him with an old leather shoe and rawhide to chew on to satisfy his oral cravings, especially when teething between three and five months. *And look out for electrical extension cords.* Many pups have bitten through these, receiving severe burns. Bones are good for dogs, but not if they splinter. A piece of thigh or shank long bone from a steer is ideal; adult dogs enjoy gnawing and it will keep their teeth clean.

Some commercial dog foods are flavored with traces of garlic or onion, substances dogs especially prize. In fact, the addition of garlic or onion may help a depressed or convalescent dog regain its interest in food. Dogs do develop specific taste preferences, refusing to eat commercial food and insisting instead on best hamburger, which is very bad for the dog if that is all it will eat because it is an unbalanced diet. It is important to start pups on a good commercial food at weaning time and rarely if ever to give them table scraps, because commercial feeds are now scientifically formulated and provide a balanced diet that no amount of scraps could equal.

Eliminative Behavior

In the dog, urine especially is used for territorial "marking" and also as a social "calling card," informing others that pass of his presence and, in turn, giving the dog information as to which dogs are around and how recently they have visited the scent post. The scraping up and ripping up of the turf with hind and forelegs after marking is not an incomplete or vestigial (catlike) burying action, but a secondary marking of the earth as an additional visual signal for all to see and perhaps to emphasize the urine mark. Males mark and investigate far more than females, although the latter show an increase in both behaviors when in heat. The urination patterns of male and female are under hormonal control. Male pups castrated when very young do not usually develop the adult leg-raising action and continue to squat in the infantile way. Females given male sex hormone will subsequently raise their leg in the male pattern. A number of normal females will raise one hind leg occasionally when urinating.

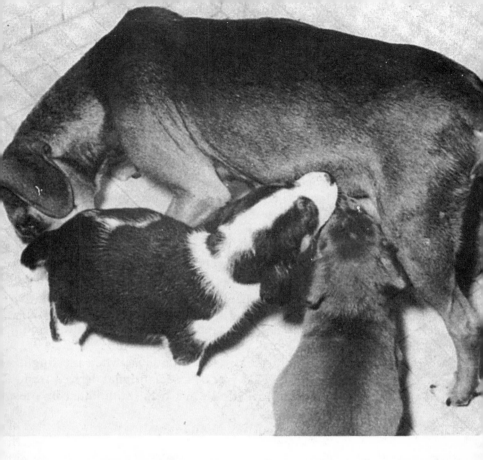

As the pups get older, the bitch will nurse them in the standing position, and she continues to clean them, during which time they remain passive

As already stated, between four and five weeks of age pups begin to leave the nest to urinate and defecate in a defined area, and this natural habit facilitates housebreaking. It is virtually impossible to housebreak those species that do not eliminate in a specific area, such as birds and sheep, for example.

Closely tied in with marking behavior is rolling and rubbing in various odors. (See Chapter 11 for further details.)

Emotional factors also influence eliminative behavior. A fearful dog will urinate, defecate and even evacuate its anal glands. These glands are situated on each side of the anus and produce a sour, rancid odor. The glands often become blocked up and have to be treated by a veterinarian, since the condition can be extremely painful for the dog. The anal gland secretion may serve normally to impart a personal "identity tag" to feces and may also advertise that a bitch is in heat, estrus possibly causing some change in anal gland secretion and in the urine, minute traces of which can be detected by male dogs.

Submissive dogs will often pass a little urine when greeting a person or superior dog. This may be a social signal derived from the infantile pattern of urinating when being stimulated by the mother.

Sexual Behavior

Mention has been made in Chapter 3 of the precocious sexual behavior patterns seen especially in young male pups. Such behavior is rarely seen in young females. It should be added that young male dogs when being petted will often show an erection. This reaction may be purely an emotional reaction to handling, at which time a number of bodily changes occur which are indicative of autonomic nervous system activity, most dramatic of these changes being a decrease in heart rate.

The age of attainment of sexual maturity varies from one breed to another, and additionally there is great variation within breeds. As mentioned in Chapter I, selective breeding has ap-

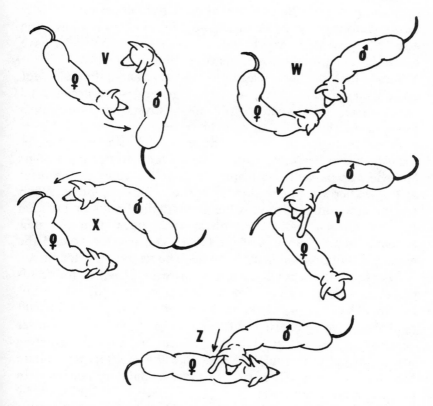

A series of typical body orientations between a male and female dog: V male gives lateral display to female, who approaches and investigates; W male turns and sniffs the mouth and ears of the female, who reciprocates; X male sniffs and licks the vulva (and anus) of the female, who is presenting (tail to one side); Y male raises forepaw and mounts; Z male raises forepaw to stand over female, who, if sexually receptive, will probably not turn and snap at him parently accelerated the onset of sexual maturity in domesticated dogs compared to wild canids that do not reach sexual maturity until two to three years of age. Also wild canids only have one estrus, or heat period, per year, while domesticated dogs have two and sometimes three heats annually.

Some dogs do show clear sexual preferences (females for certain males and vice versa), but in general such preferential behavior is not seen, there possibly being strong selection against this wild trait in the past by early breeders.

When in heat the bitch produces a chemical message, or pheromone, in her urine which will sexually arouse male dogs. She will also present and display her swollen vulva to the male and move her tail to one side when she is fully receptive. When the male mounts and clasps her around the flanks or inguinal region, she will stand motionless; with ejaculation the pair become "tied," the vulva of the female constricting around the engorged bulbus glandis of the male. The tie may last for fifteen to twenty minutes but does not seem to be essential for fertilization, because bitches can be fertilized by artificial insemination. The function of the tie is therefore unknown.* In wild canines, the male courts the female and remains with her after several copulations, sticking close to the den site and assisting her in raising the young. He will, like the mother, regurgitate food for the young. These pre- and post-copulatory behaviors in male domesticated dogs have been essentially inhibited by modern breeding practices; the female is bred by the stud without prior courtship and the male does not stay with her and tend the young. Free-ranging dogs will often show elaborate courtship behavior to females that are going into heat, however. It would be of interest to see if such behaviors are still present by allowing the male to remain with the female after copulation. Some breeders have tried this, with varying results. They find either that the stud is also a great father or that he is indifferent or even kills the pups. Clearly breeding practices have greatly affected much of the courtship and paternal behavior of domesticated dogs.

*The tie may prevent semen leakage and thus increase the chance of fertile mating.

Bitches that are not bred may become pseudopregnant ("phantom" pregnancy).

Social dominance influences sexual behavior. Thus a dominant female may not allow a subordinate male to breed, while a dominant male might be unable to breed with a very fearful female that rolls over submissively! Basically the male has to be dominant over the female (a canine downer for women's lib, but a biological fact nonetheless!).* A dominant male dog may, merely by his presence, inhibit socially inferior males from copulating.

Emotional factors are also important. A male may refuse to breed if he is fearful or in a strange place. It is primarily for this reason that the bitch is brought to the male's pen, where the latter is more confident and dominant. Some degree of passive submission in the female will not interfere with breeding to the same extent as in the male, who of course has a more active role to play.

Maternal Behavior

Toward the end of gestation the bitch will begin to seek seclusion, a safe, warm, dark and quiet place, and it is advisable to make such provisions by placing a whelping box in some corner that she will accept. Too many owners wait until the last minute to take the dog away from its usual sleeping place and put it in the basement or garage. This is just too late in the game, and few bitches will accept such treatment; complications may arise in that the bitch may actively inhibit delivery or may refuse to care for the pups or allow them to nurse. She should be shown her whelping quarters early on in pregnancy and be given plenty of time to get used to them. Just as the environment severely affects the male's sexual behavior, it can totally disrupt normal delivery of pups and subsequent maternal behavior.

Some bitches will begin scratching and whining on the linoleum or carpet and may attempt to make a nest. If a whelping box with bedding has been provided early in the

---

*But, in all fairness, a bitch in heat may mount a lethargic male and this may sufficiently arouse him to appropriately consummate the relationship.

gestation period, such final, often hysterical, reactions will be greatly reduced, if not entirely eliminated.

Bitches do occasionally cry out when a pup enters the birth canal, and some may require assurance and gentle handling. Hysterical reactions may be due to a combination of fear and pain, although hypocalcemia (a rapid fall in the blood calcium level, which can be fatal) may cause superficially similar reactions and appropriate veterinary advice should be sought immediately.

Where possible the owner should avoid any kind of handling or interference. If all seems to be going well, a bitch delivering is best left alone. The slightest interference could disrupt the normal sequence of birth and immediate maternal reactions to the newborn. The presence of a strange person may delay the delivery of pups and disrupt the entire birth process. The rule, therefore, is to keep away, observe discreetly and intercept only when 1) the bitch is hyperactive or hysterical, 2) a pup is stuck halfway out of the birth canal or 3) the bitch ignores the pups and does not a) remove the membranes, b) lick them dry or c) allow them to nurse. It is good to have a veterinarian within easy reach at such times and to have an experienced person with you for your first delivery, preferably someone the bitch knows well.

Aggressive Behavior

Breeds differ in aggressiveness, which may be based on their tolerance for proximity of others. Wirehaired fox terriers and notably bull terriers are extremely intolerant of close proximity, especially of strange dogs and dogs of the same sex. Other breeds are more tolerant, and such proximity tolerance may have been selectively bred for in pack hunting dogs such as beagles and foxhounds.

When a dog is placed in a pen with others that have formed a social group, it may be excluded, attacked or, more usually, assimilated into the group. This latter process involves readjustment of the existing social structure of the group, the social or dominance hierarchy. In some breeds no obvious hierarchy is formed, the group being essentially amorphous. In others a clear hierarchy is evident, but where proximity intolerance and competition are high, only a small social grouping of four to six or even fewer animals is possible. This is because whenever there is conflict, aggression tends to travel down the hierarchy; number one bites number two, who cannot bite number one and instead redirects his frustration to number three, who in turn bites number four, and so on. Thus the dog at the bottom of the pack receives the most redirected aggression; several individuals may even turn on him. For this reason, some breeds cannot be housed in numbers over four (two male and two female) or even over two (one male and one female). Weight and sex are important factors in determining who will be dominant, larger males usually being at the top of the hierarchy.

If a young pup, or wolf cub, is raised with adult dogs or people, it will usually remain subordinate, but if it is overindulged and permissively raised by its owner (or the companion adult dog is extremely submissive), it may assume a dominant role when sexually mature.

One common cause of aggression is territorial defense: The dog will defend its home against intruders, especially dogs of the same sex. Aggression may be reduced by castration, male sex hormones (androgens) being implicated with territorial aggression and male-male rivalry. Frustration is also a common cause of aggression in dogs, as, for example, when a dog is being restrained. Learning can play an important part here in controlling such frustration-aggression. If the dog is handled early in life, it will get used to being restrained and otherwise disciplined and will be unlikely to attack its owner or handler when it is not allowed to have its own way as an adult.

Most of what is known about brain and behavior development of the dog has been reviewed in this chapter. Although much seems to be innate or genetically controlled, it is the environment—what the pup experiences, how he is handled, and so on—that can make or mar him, even if he has the very best genetic background. In the next chapter, then, a number of procedures tested and tailored to bring out the best in a dog will be explored. By closely following some of these, the pup owner may be able to provide the best rearing environment to ensure that he will realize the full potentials of his pet.

6

Superdogs, or a Brave New Dog World: A Better Environment to Produce Better Dogs

IN THIS CHAPTER I want to focus attention on some recent experiments that have shown how environmental influences early in life can have profound and enduring effects on behavior.

Behavior is neither a product of inheritance alone nor of environmental influences or the effects of experience. As emphasized earlier, it is best to regard behavior, the phenotype, as a consequence of interaction between the genotype, or inherited capacities of the animal, and the environment. Accepting the fact that heredity plays a vital role in the development of behavior, we will consider some environmental factors which affect its progress.

Although certain environmental influences may compensate to some extent for some inherited defect such as timidity, we must consider the eugenic and ethical ramifications. With appropriate treatment early in life it may be possible, for example, to improve the behavior and emotional reactivity of a touch- or sound-shy animal. This should certainly be attempted, but if there is the slightest suggestion that the desirable trait in question is inherited, then one must seriously consider not breeding from such an animal. Too many breeders are selecting solely for conformation, for "showy" or "stylish" looks, which often become distorted, mimic exaggerations of the original breed standards. Insufficient attention is paid to selecting for stable temperament and for trainability and, consequently, many breeds are becoming suburban status symbols— ornaments, not companions. They are untrained, unworked, and no longer used for the purpose for which they were originally bred. Temperamentally they are relatively stable within the narrow confines of their suburban environment—within the house, the backyard and in the car.

An insidious change is therefore taking place in many breeds as the life-style of their owners has changed; both dog and owner are quite different from what they were only a few generations ago. Many people, as observers like Charles Reich have recently noted, are no longer people—they are human beings who in their overstressed, frustrated and unfulfilled lives are neither really "being" nor really "humane." Similarly, many dogs are no longer dogs; in modern urban and suburban life they are neither really "*familiaris*" nor really "canine." The impact that our present life-style has on us and on our pets needs a careful reappraisal, for there is urgent need for social reorganization and improvement in our way of life, as indicated by the wide and ever-increasing use of psychiatric and community counseling. Some of the problems that confront the urban and suburban dog *and* his owner will be considered in Chapter 11.

Laboratory studies have shown that there are essentially three classes of early stimulation which can profoundly influence later behavior. Each one is related to the degree of maturity of the animal at the time of stimulation. One, for example, has no effect until a particular part of the nervous system is sufficiently developed so as to be susceptible to such stimulation. Researchers speak of these as "sensitive" or "critical" periods.

The first period has been identified in rats and mice as being restricted to the first five to ten days after birth. The dog may be similar. In this first period the animals are responsive to a restricted class of stimuli—not light or sound, for they cannot yet see or hear, but scent, for they can smell, and also tactile and thermal stimuli, for they are very sensitive to touch and to changes in temperature. It has been found that if mice or rats are simply removed from the nest for three minutes a day for the first five to ten days of life and kept for this time at room temperature, their body temperature falls. This mild stress affects part of the hormonal system of the developing animal—the adrenal-pituitary system—and somehow "tunes" this system, so that animals exposed to this mild stress early in life are superanimals when they mature—"super" because they are able to withstand stress better than littermates that have not been exposed to this early stress. As adults they respond to stress in a "graded" fashion, while nonstressed littermates' response is more "all or nothing," in that a little stress for them as adults is responded to maximally. Consequently they easily become exhausted and may die if exposed to intense and prolonged stress.

For instance, if they are tied down and unable to move for twenty-four hours rats develop severe stomach ulcers, but littermates that have experienced the mild handling stress earlier in life are more resistant and do not ulcerate. Both male and female rats attain sexual maturity sooner if they have been stressed early in life. They are also more resistant to certain forms of cancer and infectious diseases and can withstand terminal starvation or exposure to cold much longer than littermates that have not been so stressed. The EEG (brain electrical activity) of cats and dogs matures faster if they have some degree of stress early in life and, because they are less emotionally disturbed than nonstressed littermates, they perform much better in certain problem-solving tests later in life. At the present time we do not have sufficient information as to the optimal amount of stress to give young animals to make them psychologically and physiologically superior. The amount of stress and the best time (sensitive period) to administer it varies among individuals of different breeds or strains. Optimal stress for one strain or species of animal may be too intense for another and actually retard development, causing pathophysiological stress reactions rather than producing psychophysiological superiority. We must be cautious at this stage, therefore, but at least mindful of the potential of such procedures in producing superanimals.

Suffice it to say that it is undoubtedly bad practice to raise young animals—and children, for that matter—in a completely protected, insulated environment. Overswaddling and coddling may reduce stress tolerance and resistance later in life. A little stress is a good thing, but *how much* and for *how long* we have yet to discover and to formulate for different species, breeds, strains and individuals. One Russian worker, Dr. L. Arshevsky, has begun such studies on human infants, and his results so far are very promising. My own work with beagles exposed to thirty minutes of daily stimulation from birth until five weeks of age produced some very promising results but also revealed that extreme caution is necessary in order to avoid excessive stress and possible pathophysiological reactions. Stimulation consisted of administering a wide variety of stimuli, such as brief cold exposure, cutaneous stimulation by stroking, stimulation of the balancing organs of the nervous system (the semicircular canals) by gently tilting and rotating the pup and stimulation of the visual and auditory systems by electronic flashes and clicks. We found changes in the developing heart rate and in the adrenal glands that indicated we were actually producing physiological stress. It is possible that even more severe stress could cause adrenal exhaustion and increased susceptibility to disease.

Our handled pups, however, were far more active and exploratory than their nonhandled littermates, over which they were invariably dominant in competitive situations. In a learning test in which the pup had to solve simple detour problems, the nonhandled pups were extremely aroused, yelped a good deal and made many errors. They were clearly more emotionally disturbed in the test situation than the handled pups. The latter kept their cool, making few errors and solving the problems very quickly and with little distress vocalization.

We are not yet in a Brave New World of genetic engineering and selective breeding in human beings, although we practice the latter on our dogs with some degree of success. It is quite remarkable that only until recently there has been so little attention focused on *beneficial* environmental influences in really developing the full genetic capacities of animals—or of man, for that matter. Attention has instead been directed to the harmful effects of inadequate stimulation and handling, inadequate mothering, "institutionalization" of orphanage children, and so on. One exception is Dr. Stella Chess, who uses a battery of tests to determine the basic temperament of two- to three-month-old infants. With such knowledge, the best ways to raise an infant

AVERAGE BUTLER BOX PRESS RATES PER HOUR
(1 hour pre-test habituation)

II		CI		CCI	
WINDOW OPEN (1-Hr.)	CLOSED (1-Hr.)	OPEN	CLOSED	OPEN	CLOSED
3. 0 (0-15)	0 (0-1)	12. 5 (1-52)	13. 0 (1-27)	27. 0 (15-56)	57. 0 (0-300)

24--MF--75

When placed in a lightproof box, only the CCI pups that have had early socialization with dogs will press a lever to open a window shutter in order to see other dogs in an adjacent pen. Hand-raised pups show hardly any social motivation, even when the shutter is left open and the number of nose presses against the open window are counted. The pups weaned at 3 weeks (CI) tend to be intermediate. Early social experiences clearly influence later social motivation

can be decided on so that individual defects or weaknesses can be compensated for (such as overemotional reactivity). In essence, the optimal rearing conditions can be tailored to the needs of the infant which are reflected in its temperament or nervous makeup, as revealed by Dr. Chess' tests.

This brings us to the next two issues, which are extremely relevant in relation to the production of superdogs (or better dogs, if you wish) and in preventing both dogs and children from being emotionally or intellectually impaired later in life as a consequence of inadequate or suboptimal early experience.

First, the issue of socialization, which is the name given the process by which infants become emotionally attached, first to their mothers, then to their peers and to other outsiders. Two things can go wrong at this stage (say, from three to twelve months of age in human infants, and, as mentioned previously, anywhere between four and twelve weeks of age in dogs). If they do not have sufficient social contact (love, cuddling, etc.) they may not develop a firm bond and they might grow up to be aloof, distant, asocial or even antisocial or sociopathic. The other

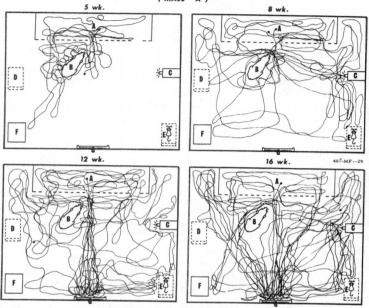

DEVELOPMENT OF EXPLORATORY BEHAVIOR IN THE DOG
(MALE - A)

Development of exploratory behavior. Activity traces of a pup placed in an arena for 15 minutes at 5, 8, 12 and 16 weeks. Activity increases, and exploration of stimuli begins (A= start box, B= toy pup, C= flashing light, D = empty rat cage, E= rat in cage, F= click sounds from a box, G= mirror). Littermates not allowed out of the home cage until 12 or 16 weeks do not explore; they are fearful of the arena (*i.e.*, are institutionalized). It is most important for pups to be exposed to an enriched and varied environment before 3 months of age

extreme is overmothering, where the mother (or owner of the dog) keeps the apron-strings tight. This overprotective rearing produces a sick, dependent offspring that is often socially maladjusted and emotionally disturbed. Neither child nor pup in this type of relationship is allowed to play, to socialize with its "dirty" peers. In dogs the situation is somewhat different in that the dog has to become socialized to both dogs *and* people. If the dog's early life is spent too close to people he may consider himself a "people dog." Such dogs, because of inadequate socialization with their own kind, are often aggressive, excessively fearful, sexually frigid or socially indifferent to other dogs. And the opposite is true as well. Dogs taken from the litter too late in life (say at four months of age) may be too dog-attached. They never seem to develop a close relationship with

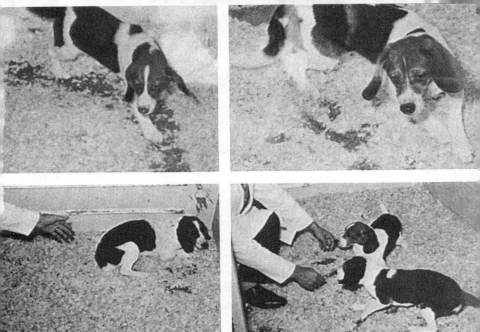

Circular pacing and whirling behavior, common stereotypes in confined dogs. These dogs were raised by Dr. J. L. Fuller in social isolation earlier in life. Note the withdrawal and fear in one of these isolates compared with nonisolated beagles

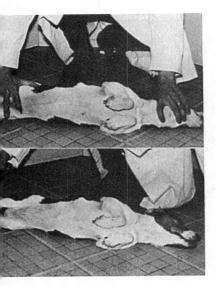

Tonic immobility, freezing or catalepsy in a beagle that has been turned onto one side, held down and then released. The animal remains rigid for several seconds. This is an abnormal fear reaction and is consistently seen in this particularly timid line of dogs

people and they are often difficult to train. Clearly, therefore, with dogs we have to strike a happy balance so that we can ensure that the dog will be well attached to both people and dogs.

The second issue is that of enrichment. Children and pups who have been raised surrounded by all kinds of interesting objects which they are free to investigate and manipulate seem to develop faster. In later life they are more inquisitive and probably more intelligent because they have experienced so much in childhood. Contrast this with the dull, underprivileged children that have had little varied stimulation during development. They are almost zombielike, having a minimal requirement for varied stimulation. The TV alone may be sufficient to keep them content all day, where a more privileged child will soon become bored and seek further increment of experience. And all the time he is learning, his developing nervous system is storing information that will be of inestimable use at some later date. We have raised dogs with various degrees of enrichment, and those that have spent the first twelve weeks of their lives in a kennel prefer to stay there and never come outside to explore. Littermates that have had only a few minutes outside the kennel in a very stimulating environment at five and eight weeks of age are very inquisitive and active by twelve weeks. Leave the kennel door open, and they come bounding out. The others that have never been free, with rare exceptions, don't venture out. They are fearful of unfamiliar objects, and instead of investigating they withdraw. A dog of superb genetic background could be ruined this way. Obviously he would be very difficult to train, for the trainer would have to spend hours helping the institutionalized dog overcome countless phobias or irrational fears. Even if he received plenty of human contact to ensure that he would be well socialized, he may still develop this "kennelosis" disorder. And if he was from a rather timid line of dogs to begin with, his chances of recovery would be even slimmer.

We have explored three very important issues which are under

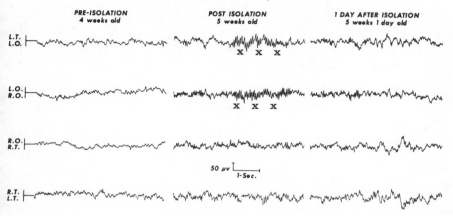

EEG RECORDINGS OF ISOLATE BEAGLE - 3
(FAST RECOVERY)

PRE-ISOLATION
4 weeks old

POST ISOLATION
5 weeks old

1 DAY AFTER ISOLATION
5 weeks 1 day old

L.T.
L.O.

x x x

L.O.
R.O.

x x x

R.O.
R.T.

50 μv
1-Sec.

R.T.
L.T.

24--MF--107

Brain wave activity in pup removed from solitary confinement after 1 week shows abnormal fast frequency patterns. Such overaroused pups soon recover, their abnormal EEG activity declining as their behavior is less hyperactive and disorganized. This illustrates the "overload" effect on the nervous system when a dog is placed in an unfamiliar, complex environment. A normal dog can presumably set up "filters" to dampen or inhibit this effect, but one that is innately timid or that has been raised in isolation for a long period may never be able to adapt to a more complex environment or to shifting situations

intensive investigation by psychologists and psychiatrists alike. They have used animals in their studies, and although their ultimate goals are to understand the processes involved and to improve *human* development, much of what has been discovered so far is relevant to dog rearing. To construct any programmed rearing schedule to produce superdogs or superhumans will entail many setbacks. It must at least be flexible enough to cater to individual and breed (or racial-cultural) differences in man and animal. In reality, we will never actually produce super beings. We will be simply providing the best environment for the individual's genetic potentialities to be brought out and completely developed. We have so far in no way fully explored, fathomed or developed the innate, latent capacities of either dog or man.

Early handling, socialization and environmental enrichment can influence both trainability and learning ability. In the next chapter, some general aspects of animal intelligence will be reviewed, with particular emphasis on the "canine IQ."

7

Animal Intelligence and
The Canine IQ

"SURELY DOGS AREN'T really intelligent . . . their behavior is purely instinctive. . . . They might be trainable, but that is no mark of intelligence." I often overhear such remarks in supposedly well-informed circles. For various reasons, scientists and laymen alike tend to shy away when the conversation gets around to comparing animal and man. Anthropomorphizing, we are taught, is unscientific; at one time it was also considered a heresy. Some people, in spite of their education and religious background, still object to any comparison's being made between animal and man, primarily because of their own egotism. To wit, man is omnipotent. One scientist, Lloyd Morgan, set up a canon several decades ago stating that any observed piece of animal behavior should be interpreted at the simplest or lowliest level. This parsimonious law emphasizes that we should not interpret a given piece of animal behavior as revealing a high level of evolution or of complex organization of the nervous system. This is good advice, for all of us are guilty of projecting our own feelings, reactions and perceptions in trying to interpret how an animal behaves.

But this is where the sciences of psychology and ethology have played such an important part in expanding our knowledge of animal behavior. The "objective" scientist is trained not to interpret subjectively what an animal perceives or what it might be thinking. Sometimes, though, he is stuck and against his training rather than against his better nature has to unbend and look for some higher function, possibly akin to thought processes and emotional reactions common to both animal and man. Or he may remain receptive and reserve comment until all the facts are in. I for one keep an open mind about dogs and people that show evidence of ESP, telepathy, and psi-trailing or psychic location of where another person is. I also reserve my judgment about "talking" and "life-saving" dogs. The few cases that I have looked into are often poorly documented, and what the dog has done can be interpreted at a very simplistic level rather than at the high level of introspection and superintelligence that local newspapers may sensationally assume.

But still many reports certainly suggest that under special circumstances dogs may show unprecedented insight or some "sixth sense." Witness a few examples, not really of superintelligence in other animals, but of superspecialization. The male silkworm moth can detect the presence of a female even if she is two miles away. His antennae are supersensitive to her odor, and indeed they are insensitive to anything else. They are specialized female-detectors. Similarly male mosquitoes are able to locate females because their antennae are supersensitive to the vibrations of the females' wings. They do not pick up the vibrations of the males' wings, which are of a lower frequency. Without a careful study of how a male moth or mosquito locates its mate, we might endow them with some superior intelligence, while in fact they have evolved a highly selective sensing mechanism. The same holds true for the remarkable abilities of bats and dolphins to use their own voices like sonar to locate solid objects, especially their prey. This is not superintelligence but a remarkable phenomenon of evolutionary specialization. The complex language of the dance of the bees is another example, and bees are sensitive to ultraviolet light.

The more we study animals, the more we discover how different their perceptual worlds are. What we see, hear and smell is very different from what the dog perceives. For instance, dogs are color-blind. On the other hand, to us a dog whistle at 30,000 cycles per second is inaudible, for our upper limit of hearing is around 18,000 cycles per second. But unlike many insects and such other specialists as bats and dolphins, men, monkeys, and dogs are relatively unspecialized, at least as far as we know. Dogs do, though, have a keen sense of smell which, unlike the senses of sight and sound, is well developed at birth so that they are capable of learning even at this early age.

Intelligence might be defined as the ability to use or call on past experiences in adapting to a new situation or in dealing with a new problem. As the late Dr. T. C. Schneirla of the American Museum of Natural History has emphasized, intelligence is not efficiency in adaptive behavior, for all living animals reveal this. They avoid excessive cold, heat, pain and so on. Intelligence is an ability which an individual inherits from its species—a capacity which is indeed innate or genetically determined but which has never been measured completely in man or animal. The innate potential of intelligence cannot be measured, because intelligence as it develops is affected by the environment—by the experiences an animal has as it matures. To say that one breed of dog is more intelligent than another is absolute nonsense. Drs. Scott and Fuller, for example, in their extensive studies of several breeds, conclude that they are of very similar intelligence provided that in the intelligence tests used one allows for such things as differences in physical size, agility, stamina, sensory abilities and emotional reactions which may interfere with performance. An extreme example would be to assume that after attempting to train a basset hound and a saluki to leap over hurdles the saluki has more intelligence because it made fewer errors. Similarly, the conclusion that an Afghan hound is of inferior intelligence compared to a German shepherd because the shepherd performs so well in obedience trials after only a few lessons while the hound needs countless lessons is totally unfounded. The shepherd may simply be more trainable than the Afghan hound, but trainability is not a direct measure of intelligence.

One breed of dog might have some superior sensory ability such as keen ear or nose. To compare this in terms of which is the more intelligent with another breed that might have a good eye would be spurious. The question is—like our moths and bats—which is the more *specialized* and therefore the more suitable for a particular task. (Indeed, it might be undesirable to have superintelligent dogs, for few would tolerate the ridiculous things that they are sometimes trained to do!) A moderately intelligent dog that is extremely trainable and willing is perhaps the ideal canid. Obedience, however, like trainability, is not a sign of intelligence, and obedience training to stay, sit, retrieve, and so on are not measures of intelligence per se. Using the specialist traits of the dog, such as its ability to follow a trail and to discriminate different odors, the trainer can school his dog to make extremely fine discriminations and to ignore false scents. It is on the basis of such innate abilities—the substrate of intelligence, coupled with sociability, obedience and trainability— that the dog has become man's closest companion, friend and working partner.

Intelligence is influenced indirectly by such things as emotionality and early experience. An extremely overfearful dog is much harder to train than a more "balanced" individual, but one who is too phlegmatic and easygoing may be unsuitable for certain tasks, such as guiding the blind. A dog that has had a wide range of experiences during the formative period will be motivated to seek out a more enriched environment later in life. Paced increments of experience are beneficial, and the dog with such experiences will be able to cope with complex situations at maturity; he will also be easier to train and much more reliable temperamentally. An innately shy dog will similarly tend to avoid new things and will literally rear itself in a self-restricted environment. By withdrawing from everything it will never learn about anything, it will never develop new associations and its increments of experience will be near zero.

A dog that has not been properly socialized, not sufficiently "bonded" with its owner early in life, is often harder to train than a well-socialized dog. Socialization clearly influences trainability rather than intelligence. I once worked with a strain of beagles that were not well socialized, and some of my students have attempted to train some of my wild canids, such as golden

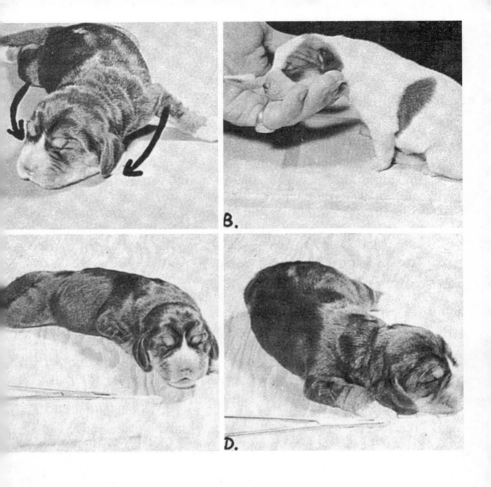

Evidence for learning in day-old pups: Side-to-side exploration (A), which is followed by direct forward crawling toward a Q-tip soaked in anise oil in (C); the mamary regions of this pup's mother had been smeared with oil at the time of delivery and the pup becomes "imprinted" onto the odor; a littermate, "roots" into the experimenter's hand more vigorously when the Q-tip is near (B); and a pup from another litter not exposed to anise, turns away and shows strong avoidance of the Q-tip stimulus (D)

jackals, that were socialized only to me: They seem to learn nothing and they are well-nigh untrainable. It would be easy to pass them off by saying that they are stupid, but, in reality, they are literally untrainable.

Some might seize on this and say that if I feel that some breeds of dog differ genetically in their intelligence, then I am supporting the racist notions that have affected mankind for generations. I would agree that some breeds *as adults* might have a lower IQ than other breeds. But this difference stems from the way they have been reared and trained. An adult laboratory beagle compared with a guide dog is as different as chalk from cheese, basically not because of genetic differences but because the guide dog has been educated while the beagle has been deprived of varied experiences and any kind of training and often even of affection. Recent work has shown that European-raised Jews have ᴀ much higher IQ (105) than Jews raised in the Middle East (85). And yet the European Jew and the Middle Eastern Jew raised on a kibbutz have the same IQ of about 115! So much for genetics; the difference is *environmental.* Are the Stone Age aborigines of Australia clearly genetically inferior to the Aryans? Culturally perhaps, or rather technologically, but genetically in terms of intelligence they may be less inferior than the racist might care to accept. Their children who have been educated by missionaries have graduated from Oxford. If there is a genetic difference in intelligence, then we have obviously not developed the best or optimal environment in which the full genetic capacities of our own children can unfold. The idea, therefore, that certain races of people or breeds of dogs differ in their innate intelligence is scientifically untenable, unproven. And it remains so, for we have not yet fathomed or developed the full genetic capacities of any breed or race through environmental programming early in life. Perhaps the geniuses that we have seen throughout history and the superdogs of legend and myth are really everyday, "average" men and dogs with the same innate intelligence, the same basic capacities as our own. But they have been raised and constantly exposed to an environment conducive to the fullest flowering of their genius, which lies dormant in the majority of their fellow species.

There are, however, specialist breeds of dogs and specialist races or tribes of men, comparable in a sense to the highly evolved specialist bats, bees and moths mentioned earlier. Man has evolved specialist traits, some genetic (physiological), others cultural, to adapt to particular climates such as the Arctic, the desert or the tropical rain forests or to the stressful urban environment. Similarly man has, through artificial selection, developed certain breeds of dogs which, like the various races of man, share identical basic characteristics yet differ on the basis of a few specialist traits such as enhanced trail-following ability—a superior nose or a good ear or eye. These are innate traits or characteristics, the frequency of which is increased by artificial selection in certain breeds.

Other "natural" traits may be enhanced or exaggerated through natural selection so that their frequency is extremely high—indeed, characteristic of a particular breed. Thus we see pointing in a more exaggerated form and in more individuals of the pointer breeds than in poodles or fox terriers, which also point but less obviously and less frequently. Thus different breeds of dogs, like different races and cultures of man, differ in the degree to which they use their sense organs and in the way in which they display, move and communicate nonverbally. The anthropologist E. T. Hall has elegantly discussed these issues in his recent book *The Hidden Dimension*. He also points out that there are cultural differences in our tolerance for proximity with our fellow men. The same is true as a consequence of artificial (genetic) selection of the various breeds of dogs. Some breeds find it difficult to endure the close proximity of others, while others, notably the pack hounds, are more tolerant. Cultural "phenocopies" in man of these genetic differences in dogs are the gregarious contact peoples of Arabia and South America (the beagles) and the noncontact peoples of North America and northern Europe (the terriers).

The above rather general discussion should be sufficient to

clarify the constant questions concerning differences in absolute intelligence and in specialist traits in man and dog. Cultural evolution, on the one hand, and domestication and selective breeding, on the other, have produced a diversity, a mosaic of similarities and of differences in both man and dog. Also a wide range of potentials lie dormant in some breeds and races, while in others they have been fully developed. Consequently one breed or race may appear superior to another, but such comparisons are erroneous. One may simply be more specialized, more perfectly adapted to a particular terrain, climate, way of life, or role.

The same holds true when we ask the question, "Are dogs more intelligent than cats?" or "Are men more intelligent than fish?" Cats are more perfectly adapted to tree climbing and fish to water; they are specialists in their own right. We might try to measure their intelligence with a few tests, as psychologists have done in the past. But the tests may favor a "specialist"; for example, a rat can learn a complex maze faster than other superior mammals, including young human beings! He is naturally adapted to mastering the layout of a particular terrain and has a great ability to learn spatial relationships between objects. This could be an insurmountable problem for a different species that specializes in a different kind of learning. Squirrels and foxes, for instance, must have a good place-learning ability, for in nature they learn where their food caches are, or at least a rough approximation of their location, while a browsing animal such as an antelope or cow, never having evolved this particular learning skill or aptitude, might perform poorly in a learning test of place remembering.

Similarly, in man "standard" IQ tests have recently been demonstrated to be of value only for the particular culture or average middle-class socioeconomic group for which they were developed. To use the same test to rate "intelligence" in different groups is pointless. All that can be shown is that groups do indeed differ, not in intelligence per se, but in specialist abilities and also in "general" knowledge, which is really specific knowledge of the group from which the original tests were developed. Nor can we develop one single standard test for intelligence for our various breeds of dogs. Tests for learning ability and trainability, yes, but absolute tests for intelligence could endorse notions of racial superiority or breed superiority, which are completely unfounded scientifically. The rearing history of the subjects must also be considered, for some patterns of child rearing in some cultures may restrict the children's development so that a lower IQ is evident.

Differences in intelligence per se have been demonstrated by comparing the learning abilities of various animals such as fish, mice and monkeys. Chimpanzees can perceive complex relationships about as well as a three-year-old child. Animals generally lack abilities to abstract and to deal with relations between abstractions. These abilities are more or less unique to man, who is also almost exclusively endowed with abilities of self-reactive reasoning, foresight and time-binding or reasoning with reference to problems in the distant future. These abilities are extremely primitive in both dog and chimpanzee. The late Professor Wolfgang Köhler, who spent many years studying the learning abilities of chimpanzees, was, however, able to demonstrate *insightful* behavior in some chimps. A subject unable to reach some bananas would suddenly switch from random behavior and come up with an immediate solution; he would stack up boxes or slot poles together (that he had previously manipulated in an aimless way) so that he could get at the bananas! Great dexterity coupled with such insightful behavior, plus the ability to learn from others through imitation, makes the chimpanzee an extremely intelligent animal.

Dogs and cats are certainly limited because they are far less dexterous, yet both dog and cat can learn through imitation and they have a good memory for place learning and are very skilled at making visual discriminations. I have heard of one dog that showed insightful behavior comparable to Kohler's chimps. This dog suddenly solved the problem of getting over a gate between the kitchen and living room (where he was not supposed to go) by moving a small stool over to the gate, which enabled him to surmount the obstacle with ease! Dogs can learn to manipulate

Dog behind plexiglass screen (above) watches where the experimenter puts food—in one of two boxes. He has to remember where the food has been put. A solid screen is then slid over the plexiglass screen for some time before the dog is released. This is called the delayed response test and is one of the best "memory tests" for dogs

This modified Wisconsin General Testing Apparatus (below), originally designed for monkeys, is also useful in testing the learning abilities of dogs. The dog has to make the right choice (discrimination); otherwise the tray is withdrawn and he gets no food reward. When the dog noses the dome-shaped stimulus, he is rewarded. The test here is one of shape discrimination

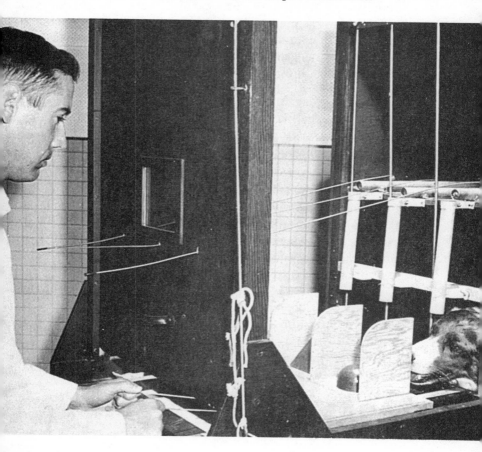

levers and to press bars for reward, but they are incapable of assembling tools as the chimpanzee can; so the question remains—are dogs more intelligent than their inferior motor abilities would lead us to believe?

Some animals in nature use tools of various kinds. Chimps will use twigs to "fish" for termites and sticks as weapons against larger predators such as leopards. One species of Darwin's finch on the Galapagos Islands uses a cactus thorn to spear grubs from inaccessible crevices. The sea otter will lie on its back with a flat "anvil" pebble on its chest and use another stone to beat open abalone shells to get at their delectable meat. Similarly, various birds such as the European thrush will use a particular stone as its anvil against which it breaks open garden snails.

Some of you may have seen carnival shows of monkeys or pigeons playing a piano or even competing in a soccer match. These animals are not showing superior intelligence or insightful behavior; they have simply been conditioned to perform a series of irrelevant acts in order to get a food reward. These acts are strung together by the trainer, so that to the observer the sequence looks like a formidable performance. A rat can be trained to release a rope ladder, climb down it, jump over a hurdle, let down a drawbridge and fire a cannon when you put a dime in the box which activates a red light which is the signal for the rat to perform. His final goal is not firing the cannon but a tiny pellet of food that is dispensed after he has fired. The food is not dispensed if he does not go through the entire sequence, so that the rat who just runs and fires the cannon when the red light goes on is discouraged from "cheating."

But very often an "instinctive drift" occurs, where the animal tends to revert, in spite of careful training, to his natural behavior. For example, a pig that is given a food reward after it has picked up wooden disk "pennies" and placed them in a large piggy bank may eventually "short out" and start holding onto the pennies and chewing on them. A chimpanzee will work for poker chips as tokens which it can then trade for food. They have the ability to make such associations and can even learn that a yellow chip is worth more than, say, a green one. To a limited extent, a dog can make this type of association. He is able to initiate the secondary stimulus by bringing his leash when he wants to go out for a walk.

Animals are extremely perceptive, and a skillful trainer can make his audience think that his animals possess superior intelligence—that they can count, do complex mathematics, and so on. The trick is simple. The trainer gets his dog, horse or elephant to nod its head or foot repeatedly until he gives a very subtle and imperceptible signal; he may raise his eyebrows, smile or move his hand slightly. Many people encountered the legendary horse Clever Hans, to whom they would give some difficult mathematical problem. Hans would start tapping his hoof and stop when he came to the answer because he was able to detect a subtle signal from his trainer or a slight change in body tension in some of the observers when he had given the correct number of taps! As emphasized earlier, we should always have an open mind but temper our interest with skepticism, for a simple answer may underlie an apparently remarkable feat!

But there still remain some uncanny feats that defy our rational minds—cases of dogs and cats being lost or abandoned somewhere and then after many weeks suddenly finding their owners who have moved to a completely new home. Some animals, by a "sixth sense," find their way to their old home when the owners move house and pet to some distant place. This "sixth sense" of animals will be discussed in depth in the next chapter.

There has been recent speculation about "smart pills" and hopes that certain drugs might increase intelligence. Some drugs such as caffeine, amphetamine and benzedrine do improve problem-solving abilities by making the subject more alert; learning and recall might also be improved. Caffeine and amphetamine, for example, have been found to improve a dog's ability to follow a trail. But as yet there are no pills that will increase the IQ. Some recent work with flatworms (planarians) has, however, shown that memory may be profitably transferred from one worm to another. If a flatworm that has learned to go through a maze is chopped up and fed to another, the cannibal learns the maze much faster! Some memory substance (memory RNA—ribonucleic acid) is thought to be involved. Come the day when we will, on the basis of flatworm science, revert to tribal cannibalism and eat each other's hearts or livers for strength and brains for intelligence! Until then we will "pick" each other's brains and benefit from the experiences of others through verbal and written transmission of information—the process of cultural transmission that makes man supreme and unique as a species.

I should mention two other points relevant to our understanding of intelligence. Dogs, cats and monkeys respond to a mirror, as do chimpanzees and people, but so far, only people and chimpanzees show self-recognition. Other animals tend to show species-recognition but do not seem to realize that it is their own reflection in the mirror. Apparently only chimps and human beings will use the mirror to groom themselves. If a red spot is painted on a chimp's head after he has had plenty of experience with a mirror, he will immediately finger the spot, while lower species of monkey will not respond.

The second point is one of esthetic perception, which Dr. T. C. Schneirla has discussed at some length. He feels that there is evidence for a primitive esthetic perception in primates, for they will spontaneously paint with clay, drape objects such as leaves or banana skins on their bodies, engage in hand-in-hand dancing and drum on a log. Desmond Morris, in his studies of painting by chimpanzees, suggests that some definitely show esthetic appreciation in the colors they select. It is doubtful, however, that dogs have an esthetic sense, although they will seek out a soft couch, a warm place in the sun and avoid raucous music. They may, though, have a sophisticated esthetic appreciation for certain odors which we certainly do not share; they delight in rolling in carrion and other materials that we find repulsive but that they consider extremely attractive. Some of my friends, after all, are repulsed by my esthetic appreciation of ripe cheese and well-aged pheasant! My wolves certainly appreciate perfumes and aftershave lotions and become ecstatic when I allow them to rub against my shaved and lotioned chin! I recall a science fiction story in which a spaceship bearing human beings crashed on an alien planet. They were found wandering in the jungle by the resident aliens and were caged and exhibited in a zoo. The earth men tried every conceivable way of communicating to their captors that they were intelligent beings, but they were singularly unsuccessful. Then one day, quite by accident, they caught a mouse. They made a cage for it and the aliens then realized that they were exhibiting "animals" in the zoo that had an intelligence on a par with their own, and so our earth men were released. I often wonder when I see our cousins—gorillas and chimpanzees—wasting away with nothing to do in the sterile cages that most zoos provide. How inhumane to sentence them to a life of solitary confinement, or absolute boredom or the hell of being with an incompatible mate. So I crawl back into my own cage and wonder if I should let my mouse go free. I think of those intelligent apes and wish that one would build a cage and put a mouse inside it. It is so difficult for them to communicate with us!

8

The Sixth Sense of Dogs

IN CONTRAST TO the disciplined, scientific study of animal intelligence reviewed in the preceding chapter, we will now venture into the little-explored world of the sixth sense.* Much has been written and speculated on, but there has been little scientific study of phenomena such as ESP and psi-trailing in animals.

Most of us have heard of at least one fantastic story of a dog's or cat's incredible journey or remarkable feat which we can only interpret as some sixth sense or extrasensory perception. For example, a family moved to a new location a couple of hundred miles away and had to leave their beloved dog with friends because they were not able to keep it in the new home. Soon they received a letter from their dog's foster home informing them that he had moped around his own home for a few days, seemed very depressed and then simply disappeared. The local humane society had no record of him, and he was presumed lost or possibly killed by a car. Some weeks later an emaciated dog appeared on the scene and was united with his family.

How did he find them? He had never been to the new home before. Some uncanny sixth sense must have enabled him to

---

* In a Ciba Company Foundation symposium on taste and smell in animals, one of the participants, Dr. Y. Zotterman, of the Swedish Research Council reported that he and another independent group of researchers had discovered infrared receptors in the dog's nose. This means that the dog, like the pit viper, can sense out warm objects and would account for the fact that while a Saint Bernard can detect a live person buried under the snow, it cannot locate a buried human corpse. The more we know about animal physiology the closer we come to an understanding of what in the past has been ascribed to a sixth sense or ESP.

accomplish this incredible feat of navigation. But what cues could he have used? His owners left no odor trail, for they left in the family station wagon. Did he "home in" on their psychic subconscious—for they often thought about him as they settled into their new home, feeling strange without a dog. They missed his presence. Is the dog capable of "psi-trailing"? A few years ago J. B. Rhine, who established the Parapsychology Laboratory at Duke University in North Carolina, did a survey of such purported cases, and these, together with the observations of the noted French naturalist and philosopher Jacques Graven in his book *Non-Human Thought,* will be discussed shortly.

First, though, I must lay a few foundation stones provided by a good deal of research on the navigational abilities of animals. Research must be conducted under carefully controlled conditions, where the necessary rigor of the objective scientist obviates a subjective interpretation of behavior that might appear magical or extrasensory in nature. It has been shown that various species of birds that migrate, often along "traditional" routes they have used for thousands of years, rely on the sun and sometimes the stars for navigation cues. Familiar landmarks are also depended on to help pinpoint the nesting grounds. But across oceans or deserts there are no such landmarks. So the bird somehow instinctively "reads" the stars and the sun. Some species may learn the migratory route from older individuals and the map is handed down from one generation to the next, although each generation relies on instinctual mechanisms that sense the approximate direction of migration. But even when there is no older generation around, the migratory pattern is somehow "wired in" to the bird's brain. At a particular time of the year he grows more active and prepares for migration. He becomes more social and a flock begins to grow. How do they know where to go? We have some idea now what cues are used— solar and stellar—and the possibility exists that the bird knows how far to go because after he has gone a given distance, his migratory "drive" may weaken and is eventually switched off approximately over the target site. But how does he compensate for the daily movement of the sun and for the flock's change in relation to the sun and stars as it moves from one latitude to another? Even man has this internal biological clock, and it takes several days for it to reset when you travel by jet from, say, New York to Paris. For a few days of adjustment to the new time, your behavior, sleep patterns and body chemistry are really out of tune with actual time, and this can cause stress. You get a cold or stomach upset. Repeated time traveling can be especially stressful, with the result that international airline pilots have to have frequent layoffs and traveling business executives are advised to avoid any serious business conferences for two or three days when they fly to Europe, or about eight days when their destination is Bombay or Calcutta!

So somehow the animal is able to use this internal time sense in navigation, but as yet science has not examined the complex machinery of the nervous system which enables animals to perform these incredible feats. Eels, for example, which as infants live in fresh or brackish water, migrate to their breeding grounds in the Sargasso Sea, from where their fry emigrate to the inland waterways where their parents grew up. This traditional migration is accomplished with no adults around to guide the young. The mind boggles at what kind of programming must be present in the brain to enable such behavior to occur instinctively without prior experience.

Consider the tiny brain of the monarch butterfly, who migrates south, lays its eggs, dies, and then its offspring migrate back to North America where the parents matured. And they pause on certain trees along the migration route that are traditional resting sites, used each year by each new generation of butterflies. American Indians venerated such trees, thinking they had some magical properties!

Salamanders and salmon migrate to spawn in the streams where they were born. To some extent they rely on a sun "compass," but they also depend on smell. They home in on the familiar smell of their natal waters, a smell to which they were imprinted early in life. Bees navigate over short distances in search of food, and scouts are able to convey information to foragers as to the direction of the food source in relation to the hive and the sun, the distance of the source from the hive and the quantity of food available by performing a complex dance. Even if it is a cloudy day and the sun is obscured, which will put off pigeons, bees can still navigate effectively because they can perceive the sun's rays through the clouds—they are sensitive to the angle of polarized light. Other great navigators, besides the migrating birds of passage and monarch butterflies, are the huge herds of migrating caribou, seals, turtles and penguins which travel through space and time along traditional paths to their breeding grounds with uncanny accuracy. Part of the "tradition" is acquired genetically as an instinctual blue print in the brain.

The sun is never shining at the same time in different places of the earth, and each square mile of earth's surface has a different relationship to it, which varies according to the time of day and with the shifts from one season to the next. If we look at the shape of the earth as it rotates on its axis around the sun, we can sketch out this relationship and draw lines between sun and earth that show clearly how the angle of sunlight hitting on one square mile differs from the angle and duration of sunlight hitting an adjacent one, even though this angle shifts according to time of day and season. Each square mile receives the sun slightly differently.

Can animals perceive this, as the Druids who built Stonehenge and other strange monolithic aggregations of stone may perhaps have done? If an animal can perceive the time and regulate its activities in accordance with the time of day or the season, it should be able to find the square mile where it lives by "reading" the sun and the angle of its rays in relation to the expected value that its internal clock anticipates. Incongruity is met with motivation to reduce the dissonance between solar and internal time. And the translocated animal is able to find his square mile on the globe. Now suppose an animal inherited the need to find and ability to locate another square mile—say a small island, its breeding grounds, several hundred miles away from the square mile in which it was born. It might begin to feel the urge to leave its natal plot when it begins to notice that daylight hours are getting shorter. Suddenly another clock starts ticking within, and the animal becomes motivated to migrate until again he reduces the incongruity between where he is at the moment (in relation to the sun) and what his new clock says about where he should be at a given time and place in relation to the sun. Thus some animals, notably the birds, have become travelers in space and time; they utilize a biological technology that man does not fully comprehend and that he has only crudely approximated for himself.

Given that some specialist animals have extremely well-evolved navigational abilities, it is quite possible that other species that do not migrate, such as dogs and cats, have some latent abilities. They may possess the basic rudiments which in the specialists have been elaborated through evolutionary natural selection. Some dogs may therefore have a greater potential than others, and we can say the same thing about people. I get lost in American streets designed on the north-south, east-west grid system and rely totally on my American-born wife who, to me, has an uncanny ability to get around even strange cities. Much of this ability must be based on her early rearing experiences. Admittedly, I am less interested in my environment and tend to filter things out, often to such a degree that I can get lost anywhere very easily! I am always impressed by the farmers of the open Midwest and prairie states who always know immediately which way north or south is. They are subconsciously in touch with the position and direction of movement of the sun—far more than I am. For me, determining it is a conscious effort. Eskimos out on the flat Arctic wilderness seem to have a sixth sense. They can find their way around in the worst of blizzards. Just a few cues—the type of snow, strength and direction of the wind and perhaps a small outcrop of rock that they might uncover provides sufficient information for them to navigate with little difficulty. They have learned to become experts, to remember a few landmarks and to keep in their heads a "space map" of all these interrelated cues.

To some extent dogs, too, are specialists in their trail-following abilities. Whenever I bring a new dog home from the lab for a few days I am always a bit worried if it begins to rain hard and said dog has roamed off somewhere, because I am afraid that the scent trail from his foot pads that he leaves as he departs might be destroyed and make it difficult for him to backtrack home. Marking objects with body secretions such as with urine or feces increases in many different species of animal that are put into a new territory. This marking may assist the animal in feeling at home and in laying out set trails along which he can move with confidence to and from den, safety shelter, sources of food, water, and so on. He must eventually learn to recognize and identify the territorial scent marks of neighbors that live various distances away from him.

This is probably why a newly acquired dog or cat can easily get lost—he hasn't yet staked out his own territory or learned the odors of his neighbors. Dogs especially leave a "calling card" at communal marking posts, and a new dog on the block must certainly learn the smells of other individuals who have different but contiguous and often overlapping territories. Imagine a dog that has been transplanted some miles from his own marked-out territory. If he follows a single spiral scanning pattern, moving out in increasing circles, he will pass through and along the edges of many strange territories until he eventually hits a neighbor's, and from then on he can proceed directly home. If he is transplanted a much greater distance away, he may only use this homing pattern when he has covered sufficient distance using solar navigation much as a homing pigeon does. We don't as yet know for sure if some or any dogs are capable of doing this. Judging by how quickly a cat will find his way back to his old home when his owners move to a new place on the other side of town, one is forced to conclude that he must not use the time-consuming spiral pattern but set off in a known direction. When fairly near home he could make finer adjustments by virtue of his sense of smell and familiarity with neighbors' territories. But how does he know which direction to go? How does a pigeon know which way to go when released several hundred miles off?

The farther away from home, the easier it should be, up to a point. Two hundred miles away his internal clock should tell him that there is an incongruity between the time that he "feels" and the time of day the sun registers by virtue of its position. He then sets off in a direction that will reduce this internal and external time difference. If the animal is only a few miles from home, he would need a much more sensitive perception of internal and external time differences, and, indeed, this seems to hold up

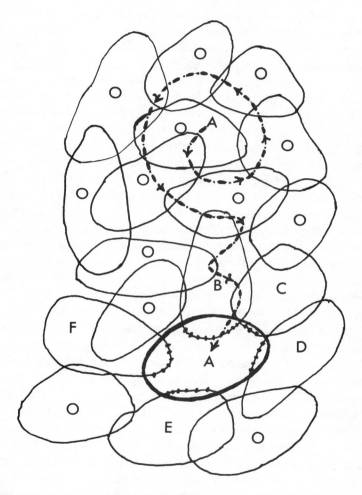

This diagram shows how a dog, removed from his territory A, could eventually find his way home if he took a spiral path from the point where he was dropped off. Eventually he would hit a familiar neighboring dog's territory B, and once he hit adjoining dog C's territory, clearly scented with the resident's urine marks, he would soon be able to find his own home territory. Note how neighboring territories of dogs B to E overlap his territory, and our dog A would certainly know the odors of these dogs and the approximate layout of their territories in relation to his from what is known about individual differences in homing pigeons. Some are really good at getting home fast when released a short distance from home, and others are very poor on short distances but do well if released a long way from home. But most pigeons on a cloudy, sunless day will do badly and might never return. They need to check local sun time with their internal clock that has been tuned to the sun time where their home is!

Behavior research seems to be getting to the root of the mystery of animal navigation, but what about the dog Prince who somehow crossed the English Channel during World War I and found his master in the trenches? Here we move into the touchy area of psychic communication, or ESP, where most scientists draw the line and skeptics support them. We should keep an open mind—that's what a good scientific investigator usually tries to do—and let's look at the evidence and sort out the facts. I lost a male Siamese cat on our farm out in the country, and I thought after many days that he had returned to our old home in the town a few miles away. We did find a very weak and emaciated male near where we lived. He was friendly and we were pretty certain that it was Igor. He had a slight squint and a twist in his tail and would come when we called his name. So we took him home. About two weeks later the real Igor appeared at the farm, half cat, half scab and skeleton. He'd probably had a tough time with a raccoon or something. I learned from this how easy it is for one to mistake the identity of one's pet, especially if it is in poor condition after a long journey or undue hardship. So one important criterion is that the pet should have some clearly identifiable mark—a collar or a really unusual spot of color. A kinky tail and squint in a Siamese cat are hardly unique! This absence of specific identifying marks was the reason many of the cases investigated by Dr. J. B. Rhine were discredited. Other alleged cases of psi-trailing were ruled out because the dog or cat in question was not far enough away and could have reached its goal by random wandering or spiral circling until a familiar scent was picked up.

Having focused in detail on how your pet may be able to find his way home, I will now mention a few apparently well-authenticated cases of psi-trailing. I should add that two other interesting categories of unusual behavior in pets discussed by Jacques Graven include the animal's having foreknowledge of a danger threatening either itself or its master and the animal's being able to foretell the unexpected return home of the master. The case of the Persian cat Smoky that Graven reviews is intriguing. This cat had an identifiable tuft of reddish hair under its chin. While his home was being moved from Oklahoma to Tennessee, Smoky was lost at a roadside stop 18 miles from the Oklahoma home. A couple of weeks later, neighbors saw the cat prowling around its old home for several days. Approximately one year later the cat appeared at its owner's new home in Tennessee, some 300 miles away!

A mongrel dog named Tony was left in the care of friends because his owners had moved from Illinois to a town in Michigan some 225 miles away. Somehow, six weeks later Tony, wearing an identifying collar, turned up at their Michigan home!

But some pets go the other way. A cat called Mastic did not like its new home in Sainte-Genevieve-des-Bois and, according to Graven's research, this same cat appeared nine days later at its old home in Buxieres-les-Mines, some 165 miles away.

Another amazing case is that of a two-and-one-half-year-old dog, Bobby, who belonged to a florist in the town of La Ferte-Alais. He got lost at the flower market in the heart of Paris and had only been there twice before. After careful searching, his master gave his dog up for lost and returned home. Yet five days later a muddy and exhausted Bobby was sitting on the doorstep! He had covered some 35 miles, but more amazing was the fact that this country dog was able to survive and pick his way out of Paris, one of the most frenetic cities in the world!

So much for incredible journeys. I have cited a few examples, but there are many, some well authenticated by witnesses and clear identification of the pet.

I don't like to end this chapter leaving the question of dog-psi hanging in the air without any scientific validation, but at this time what else can I do? All I can say is that we still have a great deal to learn about animal and human behavior and that while we should be skeptical, we should also encourage free inquiry and more rigorous study of this fascinating subject.

9

A Dog's Body Language
(and Daniel's Dilemma in the
Dog's Den)

IN THE PRECEDING chapter, the possibility has been entertained that dogs have a sixth sense and the ability for extrasensory communication. The question remains open, but there is no doubt that dogs can communicate wordlessly, using body language.

From fish to man we find a "silent" communication system composed of subtle movements of certain parts of the body—tails, fins, arms or legs. Certain postures or attitudes may be assumed in which appendages, head and trunk may be inclined in a specific way to convey a specific meaning.

"Higher" animals, generally those with fur and, of course, the Naked Ape himself, have also evolved complex and subtle facial expressions which are part of the nonverbal repertoire. The chimpanzee has at least sixteen different facial expressions and the wolf, the most highly developed social carnivore, has fourteen.

Some of the body language of the dog will be familiar to the reader, and although my interpretations are not meant to be absolute, I hope to clarify some of the subtleties of canine communication which may easily be misinterpreted. My conclusions have been drawn from detailed study of the development of this "language" in dogs of many breeds from birth onward. Some insight has also been gained from comparative studies of body language in relatives of the dog that differ in the degree to which they have evolved as social or cooperative animals.

135

From the solitary red and arctic fox to the permanent pairing coyotes and jackals to the gregarious wolves there is an ever-increasing complexity and subtlety of body language. The most social have the most elaborate silent language, and it is valuable to have this evolutionary evidence when we attempt to study the domesticated dog. Because what is a typical or representative dog—a dingo, a mongrel, a poodle? There are so many different breeds, some with no tail, others with long, pendulous ears or lips that can hardly be moved, and some with hair all over the face that effectively masks most facial expressions.

Two things should be mentioned here. First, the less social canines—the foxes—produce much stronger odors than do wolves or dogs. It seems, therefore, that odors are extremely important for communication in canines that rarely meet up with each other outside the breeding season.

Second, there is a vocal repertoire of whines, howls, growls and barks that are directly tied in with body language. These vocalizations do not, with few exceptions, carry any special message akin to words. They generally indicate an individual's emotional state—be he aggressive, submissive, needing attention or in painful distress. The equivalents in man are aggressive grunts, pain-evoked yells or screams, and so on. These emotional overtones get built in as a paralanguage to what we are saying verbally. Man does not talk like a machine but adds color or emotion in the way he intones and inflects. This paralanguage in man is clearly part of his ancestral past, and in some circles it is considered naive, unsophisticated and immature to put much feeling into what is said.

Dogs have a few vocalizations that can act as signals and therefore, since they have message value, are like words. A dog's growl and bark warn his owner of an intruder, and a bark by a female wolf will send her cubs running for cover.

But man does not communicate by words alone and this is one reason why he intuitively understands many of the nonverbal signals of animals. Dogs communicate mainly in silence, and some of the "words" and "sentences" of their fascinating body language have not been explored up until now.

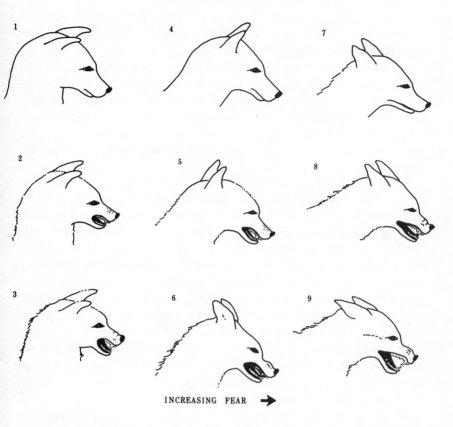

INCREASING FEAR ➡

Successive shifts in the intensity of the facial expression give information as to how aroused the animal is: From 1-4-7, there is increasing fear or submission, the ears flattened against the head and the lips pulled back horizontally to form the submissive grin; from 1-2-3, increasing aggression is displayed by erect ears, hackles and by the corners of the mouth being pushed forward while the lips are retracted vertically to form a snarl; from 3-6-9, the signals of aggression are combined simultaneously with those of fear or submission. The expression in 9, comprising the combined elements of 7 and 3, is typical of the fear biter

Besides giving some information about a dog's internal state—how he feels, whether aggressive, fearful, friendly or submissive—his body language also has a more general function. It regulates social distance or proximity between individuals. Nonverbal signals or body language displays may be broken down into two main categories: those that serve to increase and maintain social distance (such as a direct stare and a snarl), and those that serve to decrease social distance and maintain close proximity (such as low position, tail wagging and the submissive grin).

A third category, which may not be of primary communication value, includes what may be called general arousal or alerting reactions and those body postures and facial expressions seen during fear, excitement, investigation and exploration and also during certain consummatory activities, such as sleeping, scratching, drinking, eating, urinating, defecating, copulating and howling or singing. Though not meant as direct signals to others, these reactions may be perceived by one dog in another, and he may proceed to respond allelomimetically by copying the other dog. This is why dogs often tend to do the same thing at the same time. Another response to the reactions of another dog is to run over and investigate what he's doing. The intense sniffing around of one dog attracts his fellow. This is also a socially facilitated magnet effect.

These group-coordinated activities are a characteristic feature of canines that live in packs—wolves and foxhounds, for example. When there is a leader or alpha animal, it is he who most often initiates the group activity. When there is no clear leader, as in a flock of sheep, we do not see the leader-follower pattern but instead a mass effect where the action of one affects another in a chain reaction. Witness a stampede. This is termed mass or group contagious behavior and is also seen in dog and wolf packs when the pack as a whole is, for example, alarmed by a sudden noise. In less social animals housed in groups, such as the red fox, we find that such group-coordinated behavior occurs very rarely, if ever.

These group or social aspects of communication give another dimension to body language, the more specific functions of which have been briefly outlined earlier in this chapter. Consider the various signals or displays that make up this language in dogs.

DISTANCE-REDUCING SIGNALS

Your dog wants to make up to you after he has been disciplined and he behaves very much like a wolf that has been put down by the pack leader. Your dog probably feels the same way, too. He tends to avoid eye contact and often looks away in an exaggerated fashion which has been misinterpreted by Dr. Konrad Lorenz in his book *Man Meets Dog* as an intentional exposure of the throat as a sign of submission. All it really is is an exaggerated avoidance of eye contact which does, however, imply submission. The lips are usually pulled back horizontally in a submissive grin, and the ears are flattened down against the head. If touched, the dog remains completely still, and this is passive submission par excellence. The tail is tucked tightly between the hind legs and may be wagged in this low position.

Your dog will also lower his body to the ground and he may crawl forward on his belly, wagging his tail and flicking his tongue out as a licking-intention signal. If severely reprimanded, just like a subordinate wolf that has been stared down and growled at by the leader, he may look away and at the same time raise one forepaw. This is not a hand-shaking habit learned from human beings but is really a signal of the intention to roll over onto one side. And dogs do roll over as a sign of complete submission, invariably raising the uppermost hind leg and exposing the genitals just as a puppy does to its mother. And just like a puppy, your dog may then urinate. But don't punish him if he does, because it is a canine signal of absolute deference. All these signals come under the general category of "passive submission," and they may oscillate with another set of signals that have been arbitrarily grouped as "active submission" or overt friendly greeting. For example, when your dog sees you coming home he barks excitedly, wags his tail in the high position and comes bounding up to you. As you both make contact or when he reaches a certain proximity to you, his active submissive behavior gives way to or at least includes some elements of passive submission described earlier. He may roll over and urinate, or crouch down and wag his tail in the low position.

The body language of active submission or greeting includes a special facial expression which is best described as a greeting-grin, much like the human smile. It resembles the submissive appeasing grin in that the lips are retracted horizontally, but in addition the mouth is opened slightly and the angles of the lips may be pulled upward. The tongue is extruded more frequently than in passive submission and the muzzle may be jerked up-ward in much the same way a puppy will jerk its head as it roots and seizes the teat. A facial expression similar to the greeting grin is seen as a prelude to play and when the dog is soliciting play from its owner or from another dog. We can call this the play face, and it differs from the greeting grin by virtue of its intensity and by the fact that the ears are held forward and erect and panting (possibly an antecedent of laughter in man and chimpanzees) is often seen. Under such circumstances the tail is held high and wagged, while the front end is lowered so that the dog seems to be bowing down. The play-soliciting bow may be followed by alternate raising of the forepaws, which may be interpreted as an exaggerated approach. Or the dog may bow and then leap forward and give a sham play bite or a nosestab, or he may suddenly leap backward and run off, soliciting you or another dog to chase him.

Another expression which occurs during reduction of social distance is the rather rare mimic grin, which seems to be displayed, by dogs that are capable of doing it, to human beings only. The lips are vertically retracted to expose the front teeth, and at first sight it looks like an aggressive, distance-increasing snarl. This expression may be learned through mimicking human beings in those dogs that have the ability to do so.

Passive submissive posture in a coyote-beagle. Uppermost hind leg is raised to expose ventral body parts, and tail is tucked between legs. Urination often accompanies this behavior. This display is enhanced by the white chest, belly and thighs. Note also the backwards retraction of ears, narrowing of eyes and horizontal retraction of the lips to form the submissive grin

DISTANCE-INCREASING SIGNALS

The body language used to increase or maintain social distance ranges through varying degrees of threat to actual attack, and attack may range from an inhibited bite or snap at the air to a full-blown bite with a violent headshake. A typical threat display includes a direct stare and a snarl: The lips are pulled horizontally forward and vertically to expose the canine teeth, and the mouth may be opened slightly. A low growl is emitted. The ears are erect and directed forward or twisted outward and downward; in actual attack they are plastered against the side of the head, possibly to protect them.

The threat display also includes a general "enlargement" of the body in contrast to the apparent reduction of size by lowering the body in submission. Body size is enhanced by piloerection—the shoulder and rump hackles are raised, the neck is arched and the head held high, in contrast to the lowered head of submission. During attack or intense threat the head may be lowered and the neck extended, as the dog points his adversary. All four legs are stiffly extended, which again enhances body size, and the dog seems to walk on tiptoe. He may raise one leg and urinate and then scrape the ground, bristling all over and growling. The tail does some interesting things in the aggressive display. In some dogs it is arched upward and forward over the back and held stiffly, while in the wolf it is held straight and almost vertical. The tip may be wagged or flagged at high frequency and low amplitude.

All these signals of threat may be combined in different intensities, so that you can literally see how aroused the dog is and you can also predict with great certainty what his next move may be. If, for example, you move closer to him, a more intense display undoubtedly means "look out." But if his tail drops down a little and his weight shifts slightly onto his hind feet, he is probably bluffing. He might even wag his tail in the low, submissive greeting position while his hackles are still up and his facial expression is still aggressive. Here we come to an in-

A DOG'S BODY LANGUAGE

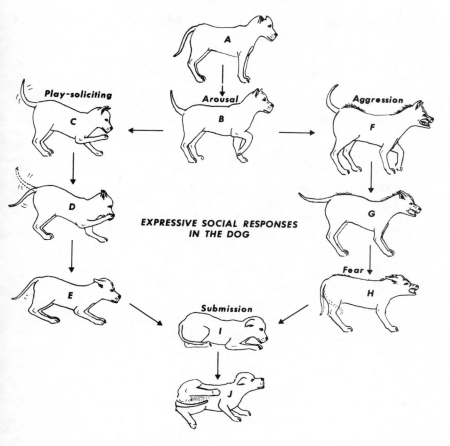

Schema of body language of the dog. A-B, neutral to alert attentive positions. C, play-soliciting bow. D-E, active and passive submissive greeting, note tail wag, shift in ear position and of distribution of weight on fore and hind limbs. I, passive submission with J, rolling over and presentation of inguinal-genital region. F-H, gradual shift from aggressive display to ambivalent fear-defensive-aggressive posture teresting aspect of behavior—the simultaneous occurrence of ambivalent or paradoxical signals.

AMBIVALENT SIGNALS

These usually occur when the dog is in some sort of conflict situation where, for example, he is at once afraid and aggressive, submissive or friendly and aggressive or afraid and yet inquisitive at the same time.

A few examples will be sufficient to illustrate how body language may express two feelings or emotions simultaneously or successively. Your dog may see something that interests him but he is unsure, even fearful. So he looks and alternatively raises and lowers his head, ears and tail; when they are up he is investigating or alert, and when they are down he is afraid. These movements are of very short duration, often lasting no more than a second, and he seems to bob up and down.

A good example of the simultaneous occurrence of signals is found in the fear-biter. Such a dog shows combined elements of fear or submission and aggression. The hackles may be up, or up partially, and the tail is usually tucked tightly between the legs. The ears are usually back in the flattened submissive position, but there is (though not always) an obviously aggressive facial expression. One reason why people get bitten is that the fear-biter can wear a submissive facial expression—ears back and lips pulled back horizontally into a submissive grin. His tail and hackles, though, may indicate that he might attack, and these other cues may not be read by the person who is concentrating entirely on the facial expression. The important thing here is to read the *whole* dog, not just his face. The fear-biter's face often displays both submission and aggression, because the submissive grin is simultaneously combined with vertical retraction of the lips so that the canines are exposed in a snarl.

The "greeting grin," here displayed by a coon hound, is a particular facial expression resembling the human grin which a few dogs can give; they seem to do it only to human beings and not to other dogs

NONSPECIFIC SIGNALS

A few signals that are not primarily for communication have been mentioned earlier, and two examples here will help complete the picture of the dog's silent language. First, when the dog is excited, he wags his tail in an upright position but the tail is carried at a very different angle and wagged at a different frequency than when he is aggressive or friendly. This excited or aroused tail wag sometimes occurs when a dog or wolf is aggressively displaying elsewhere—face, hackles, etc. This tail wagging can be misinterpreted as a playful gesture and one may suffer the unfortunate consequences.

The second example is the consummatory "pleasure" face of the dog which we see when he is scratching, rolling in some odorous material or eating. The lips are usually pulled back horizontally a little from the resting position, the ears are lowered and the eyelids are half closed. When you see this glazed expression, you will know that your dog is indeed content.

Some of the more frequently seen nonverbal signals which make up the body language of the dog have been described in this chapter. Some of the terms used are technical, but this is necessary and not just jargon—necessary because the terms are not exclusive to the silent language of dogs but also apply to that of fish and men.

A dog's body language therefore gives information as to his intentions, be they friendly or aggressive, and consequently serves to regulate social distance between individuals. This brings us to the subject of space and the concept of distance in the social world of animals and the importance of understanding just what they are expressing in their body language.

DANIEL'S DILEMMA IN THE DOG'S DEN

After being introduced to a young scientist at the Arctic Research Institute in Barrow, Alaska, I was asked my opinion, as

Dominant dog D forming an intimidating T position relative to the position of the subordinate (S) who attempts to avoid a confrontation by turning away

Direct threat stare and snarl by a dominant wolf. As in the dog, the subordinate avoids eye contact

a "wolf man," on one of the institute's wolves. It was a large black male, about 120 pounds, and my friend was intrigued by its behavior. As he advanced toward the cage, the wolf would crouch as though to pounce, but if he rushed toward the cage the wolf would back off slightly. If he then turned his back on the wolf, it would spring forward with ears erect, hackles slightly raised and tail wagging. The facial expression was not a play face with lips drawn back in a grin, but one of alert and possibly aggressive intent. But the young scientist was misreading the wolf's tail as a friendly signal, and he thought the wolf only wanted to play and wondered if it would be safe to go into the cage.

Many of us have seen a dog behind its owner's fence either showing an aggressive or alert face and yet paradoxically bearing his tail high and wagging it. In fact, these dogs, and the wolf, were showing varying degrees of simultaneous ambivalent behavior, the front end of the animal tending toward aggression and the hind end signaling some degree of friendliness. We might interpret this as a clear indication of the animal's ambivalent motivation—he wants to be friendly but he also has to defend his territory. I should add a note here—namely, that if the tail is held high, almost vertically, and is wagged stiffly and quickly, in both dog and wolf, it is an aggressive signal, and that another kind of tail wagging occurs when the dog or wolf is alert and excited by a person or even a rabbit: the tail is carried high and "flagged" excitedly to and fro.

Our black wolf was wagging his tail in this latter pattern. So with more curiosity than courage, we entered his cage. The wolf immediately backed into one corner with his tail tucked between his legs and his eyes staring at us. He neither threatened nor greeted us. The next move was up to us. I moved slowly toward him and stopped about two feet away. He gave no signal, just continued to stare. Then he defecated and that is in social situations a universal canine signal of fear—but not of submission. I advanced no farther, and he then relaxed, lay down and looked me straight in the eye. My move again. I slowly backed off, and he stood up, with that keen look on his face, and his tail went up. I quickly stepped forward again and, on cue, his

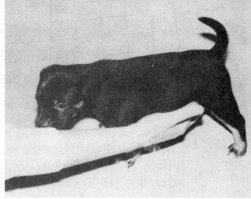

During social investigation (left), the pup on the left makes inguinal contact with the other, who remains passive. Similarly, when touched in the groin or inguinal region by a handler (right), the pup remains passive and is under behavioral inhibition or social control

Dogs of various ages will approach a painting of another dog and investigate specific body areas, including the face (F), inguinal or groin region (I) and anal (A) region. Young pups aged 8 weeks show high response frequencies to the face, and if hungry, at 5 weeks will repeatedly approach the ventral groin region of the model as though searching for a teat

tail went down and he crouched. We then backed out of the cage and closed the door and he immediately rushed at us as soon as we turned to leave.

Some of his behavior was bluff, but all of it was related to how close we were to him when we were outside and inside his cage. I have described his behavior in detail because it illustrates some fascinating things about social distance in animals, be they dogs, bears, wolves or lions. Perhaps you have all seen the dog who barks furiously as you approach, who backs off when you get very close and who again barks and may even chase you as you turn your back on him and walk away. Every mailman and delivery boy knows this pattern intimately. When we come within a certain distance of a wild animal, it begins to feel uncomfortable and moves off. If we don't advance any farther and remain quite still, the animal may then settle down and resume what he was doing. But if we move forward again a few yards, he will again move away. What we are doing is entering his *flight distance,* which is like leaping an invisible wall. If we stay outside it, the animal will not take off.

With domesticated animals we can cross this invisible barrier because they are socialized to us, although a dog that is shy of strangers will run off and in some ways, therefore, resembles a wild animal. Now if a wild animal is cornered—as in a cage— unable to escape, it may resort to defensive aggression and attack if we cross a second threshold. This is the *critical distance,* and many a dog who is a fear-biter only attacks when this invisible barrier is crossed. In socialized animals we might call this the *personal distance,* within which he will accept familiar people, and in such an animal the flight distance may be called the social distance, within which he tolerates the presence of strangers and does not run away.

With grizzly bears in the wild, one has to be cautious because the critical distance is only a little less than the flight distance. One can be at a safe distance observing the bear and he will not amble off because you are not in his flight distance. But if you move forward too fast, you might cross into his flight distance

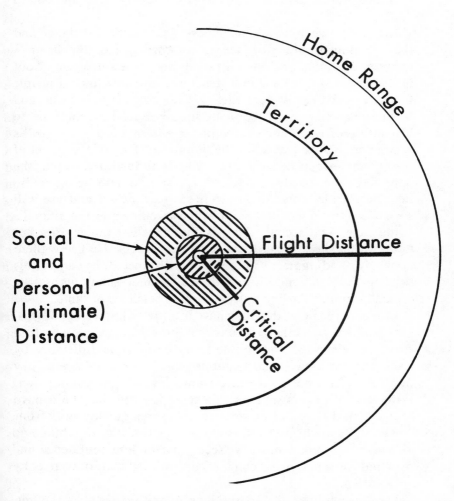

The concept of space in the animal's world: In an animal socialized to people the flight and critical distance responses are absent and a person is able to enter the social and personal spheres. An unsocialized animal will not allow the latter proximity and will run off if a stranger enters its flight distance or attack if the critical distance is invaded. Territory is regarded as the area that is defended by the animal, while the home range is the area that he covers in search of food and then into his critical distance. He suddenly turns and chases you!

Lying somewhere between the personal or critical distance and the social or flight distance is another space dimension—territory. A wolf or dog on neutral territory—in a new pen or out in the park—will behave in a less aggressive way toward people than he will on his own turf. On a stranger's well-marked territory he will most probably be submissive. These facts are to be considered when one contemplates entering a dog's or wolf's cage or in joining Daniel in the lions' den. Part of the secret of the lion tamer's success is that the ring is *his* territory, so that the lions have the disadvantage and are subordinate or otherwise inhibited. Unless his lions have been hand-raised and are well socialized, only a fool or a Saint Francis would enter the animals' home cage. The second thing is that the lion tamer does not move within the critical distance of his charges. He keeps them at bay by standing firmly in their flight distance. If he can put his head in the lion's mouth and therefore enter safely across the critical distance, the lion must be either socialized or tame.

Daniel in the lions' den may have intuitively known about this, but there are two other reasons why he wasn't eaten. The first was that he showed no fear; he kept the lions at a distance by staring them down and establishing his dominance. They therefore could have accepted Daniel as a high-ranking lion. With less social cats such as a tiger or leopard, he would have been a goner! If he had shown fear and moved quickly away from the lions, he might have released the prey-chasing, -catching and -killing chain reaction. I have seen a person lose confidence and turn and run when being challenged by a dog, and, of course, he gets bitten.

Daniel may have shared the luck of the fox's ducks though. Apparently ground-nesting ducks, and even rabbits, have been found raising their young just a few feet away from a fox's den. The fox will readily eat duck or rabbit, but possibly when they are within his den site area they may not release his prey-killing instinct. It is conceivable that the fox is not motivated to hunt when he is at home but only when he is out on his hunting range.

So Daniel and duck may rest with impunity provided they are close to the carnivores' den. We have a good deal to learn about these space- and distance-related phenomena in wild and socialized animals.

I hope that I have clarified a few of these intriguing aspects of animal behavior and that next time you decide to enter a wolf's cage, you will bear these points in mind. You will then be able to anticipate what the animal—dog, wolf or lion—might do, and if you are reading his behavior, too, you will have even greater insight.

I should mention two more relevant facts. First, an animal, be it a dog or an ape, that has been cooped up in a cage for a long time may become abnormal: He is excessively aggressive toward anyone, even a female of his own species, whom he might kill. The reason for this hypertrophy of territorial defense is obscure, but this extreme behavior is well recognized by ethologists.

The other point is that some animals from certain islands such as the Galapagos have no flight or critical distance, possibly because they have never had any predators. You can approach these wild island animals and touch them, and they neither fly away nor threaten you—and then you *do* feel like Saint Francis!

Since dogs communicate and regulate social distance in ways very similar to man, do they perhaps feel the same way toward each other and can we therefore speak of a real sense of morality or of social conscience in dogs? In the next chapter we explore the comparative morality of dogs, wolves and men.

10

The Morality of Dogs, Wolves and Men

MANY PEOPLE SAY how much they prefer the company of dogs—or of children as a second choice, perhaps—over the company of adult people. They feel more at ease, they believe that dogs are moral creatures, altogether incapable of deceit. Like children, dogs never mask their emotions but always express them openly. They are so easy to read because of their straightforward system of communication, which even a child can quickly comprehend. A child laughing or a dog wagging its tail and horizontally retracting its lips into a grin are displays that directly express what the individual is feeling. Both dog and child (the latter until perhaps about ten or eleven years of age) are incapable of disguising their feelings—feelings that are expressed eloquently in the silent language of body posture, movements and facial expressions. We can read this language and can often recognize the phony or artificial cover-up smile of an adult or adolescent. A small twitch at the corner of his mouth, a momentary furtive movement of the eyes or agitated hand gesture gives the show away. We see through the adult's masquerade and consequently feel ill at ease. The genuine openness of unsophisticated children and of dogs is certainly preferable to the company of such people who make us feel uncertain of how they really feel about us.

One of the main reasons why the dog can be such a close companion to man is that very body language, so similar to our own. And perhaps dogs can read man? My own two wolves are possibly even more expressive and totally open and honest about their feelings than are many breeds of dogs. They are also extremely attentive to my own nuances. Admittedly there are many pet dogs that also have this ability to sense their owners' moods. Some people go so far as to say that such animals must have ESP, but, in fact, they are simply superb observers. It is only man, as he matures, who appears to be capable of deceit, although I often wonder about some domesticated dogs who may seem to deceive the observer but who in reality simply cannot express themselves clearly because of pendulous ears, lips, stumped tails and hair all over their faces. They certainly cannot easily display their aggressive or friendly intentions, and I for one find it hard to detect low-intensity aggression or other weakly expressed signals of subtle shifts in emotionality that would be easy to detect in a wolf or a "clean-cut" dog.

We are fortunate that wolves and a few other dog relatives are alive today so that we may understand pure canine behavior uncontaminated by domestication. In a few remaining wilderness and conservation areas and under less ideal conditions of captivity these studies are being conducted, studies which may ultimately help us understand not only our dogs, but also ourselves. Racial and cultural differences in man, which are a product of cultural evolution, are to some extent comparable to breed differences in the dog, which are a product of domestication (selective breeding or artificial selection).

Besides the close similarities in facial expressions in man and dog, and the fact that canines and children share a total honesty, there are other similarities in the social life of canines which closely resemble the moral and ethical codes of man. Respect for another's personal distance is seen in man and dog alike. We do not stand too close to strangers, and if we accidentally bump against them in the street, we automatically apologize. People, according to their cultural background, as well as their familiarity with each other, have different personal distance. Wolves respect each other's personal distance, but the leader wolf has the greatest freedom and can "presume" on others and break into their personal spheres. Other wolves behave submissively, yet they, the subordinates, will attempt to enter into the personal sphere of the leader. They crawl on their bellies and show submission but at the same time wag their tails and attempt to lick his face.

In the various breeds of dog, we find some that are very intolerant of strangers entering their personal sphere. They will attack, often unmercifully. This intolerance is a product of selective breeding, characteristic of some terriers, and as a consequence they are less gregarious than beagles, for example. When people and animals are crowded together, all morality, dignity and principles break down if the individual's personal sphere is shattered. Some races of people, species of animals and breeds of dogs can tolerate more crowding than others, because their personal spheres or distance requirements are smaller. Man can protect his by building walls and other structures, and modern architecture does help us, for example, to adapt to crowded work conditions. But we often feel the stress, become more irritable, and our morals give way to frustration and aggression. If we placed a dozen fox terriers in a small pen, severe fighting might break out in some strains and a number of dogs might be killed, yet we might be able to keep forty beagles peacefully in the same space.

Dogs, wolves and men also react if their territories are trespassed upon. Territories include the den area and the hunting range for wolves. In nature, animals respect each other's territory, principally through fear, for the possessor or the resident pack is usually dominant—dominant only on its own territory, however, where it has the initiative. Possession is ninetenths of the law of dominance. In a stranger's territory, you are subordinate. Once established, territories space animals out and peace reigns, for there is mutual respect (or fear) of territorial rights. The wolf pack and in the Arctic domestic packs of Huskies will violently defend their territories against intruders, but they do not violate the territories of others. Similarly our domesticated dogs behave in the same way. A miniature poodle can drive away a Saint Bernard if it enters his property, and the latter withdraws discreetly, accepting the tiny resident dog's superiority. In man, these territorial rights are supported and upheld by legal rights, because the biological laws themselves are apparently insufficient to govern our own species!

Again, under conditions of more crowded living or of food shortage, animals and people will more aggressively defend their territories against impoverished, desperate intruders who violate their territorial boundaries. This is war in its most basic, biological form. But it is rare in animals; the nonbreeding nontenants usually migrate or die. In man war is now rare in this biological form; it has evolved with culture and technology into disputes over political ideals and territories that exist only in confused or distorted minds.

English law gives us some intriguing insights into the relationships between man and animal and what legal rights various domesticated animals have in society. The *Royal* Society for the Prevention of Cruelty to Animals was established at the beginning of the nineteenth century, but it was not until over sixty years later that the *National* Society for the Prevention of Cruelty to Children was founded—and not even under royal patronage. The law seems to protect dogs better than children, and British courts are notoriously lenient to child-beaters compared to the punishment they hand down when a man is found guilty of mistreating his dog!

A person cannot sue the owner of a domesticated animal that attacks him if that animal is on its owner's property. The law seems to respect the fact that the animal's territory and personal sphere should not be violated. A dog in Britain is allowed one bite. If it bites a person for the first time, its owner is not held responsible. The vicious propensity of the dog has to be proven. This seems fair treatment for the dog, for so often it is more the fault of the person who was bitten. But in countries where rabies is a problem, such leniency in favor of the dog is obviously questionable, and in the United States the laws are much more strict. The legal theory in Britain is that all dogs are human-lovers and that it is their nature not to attack people. But other animals are protected better than human beings. For if the dog attacks any horse, cow, sheep, pig or domestic bird, even if it is the first time, his owner is fully responsible. A lamb is protected better than a baby under the British legal system! The law also seems to believe that dog does not bite dog, because if your dog attacked mine, I could only get compensation if I could prove an earlier attack. A cat certainly has more freedom, for the law recognizes the natural propensity of the cat to wander onto other people's property, to kill domesticated birds, and so on. Its owner is not liable for any of its misdemeanors! Clearly *English* law places the dog in an odd position—with liberties above other animals and at times even above human beings. This legal schizophrenia is attributable to the difficulties in precisely defining what is natural and unnatural for the dog to do. He is so close to man, both socially and emotionally, and at times seems almost human and at other times like a wild animal. The law cannot distinguish between what is natural and unnatural for a dog and so finds a compromise in treating the dog above all others as a "human animal."

In the United States, the legal system varies from state to state and from one town to another. In some places there are strict leash laws and dogs are not allowed into parks, even on a leash! More rigorous legal controls on canine freedom are essential in those countries in which rabies is common, and the British Isles are fortunate in that they do not have a reservoir infection of rabies in their wild animals. Skunks, raccoons, foxes and bats are the main reservoirs for rabies in America, and it is from these wild sources that dogs become infected. The intriguing thing about English law, now operating in the absence of such a disease problem, is that it so beautifully reveals the relationship between man and dog in a formally defined cultural setting.

Wolves show mercy and compassion. When a weaker wolf loses a dispute and displays its submission, the superior's aggression is cut off. The fight ceases abruptly. Such chivalry was part of the ritual of hand-to-hand combat, but since the advent of more efficient weapons that can be used over greater distances, chivalry in war has virtually been eliminated. The soldier merely pushes a button and never sees the pain and suffering of his enemy, nor does he hear their pleas for mercy and compassion. Technology of war makes man not immoral but amoral; chivalry is dead.

Our domesticated dogs usually show the chivalry of the wolf, but often we hear of dog killing dog and even male attacking female, which has never been recorded in wolves. Certainly we must excuse some for the fact that they may be penned or crowded and unable to escape. But some dogs have been selectively bred to fight to the kill, like Spartan warriors. They show no mercy and do not respond to their adversaries' submissive pleas. Conflict ends in death. In the wolf, and in civilized man, conflict ends in some ritualized agreement. When killing occurs in man and dog we must look into the causes, which may be attributable to cultural differences and to the effects of domestication respectively. We must also consider training; we can train a few dogs (many fail) to kill, just as we can indoctrinate and educate children to kill—to kill on command, to show no mercy to their own kind.

Wolves, some men and some dogs will display their weapons but not use them. The display is a threat, a ritual between two contestants; the teeth are displayed but rarely used. The subordinate in such a cold war encounter loses face and is allowed to back off unharmed. The superior never pursues to attack him. Occasionally the superior wolf may bite a rival, but the bite is controlled or inhibited if the rival immediately submits to his dominance. What makes man or dog lose control? Suddenly the man shoots, even though the threat display of his gun is sufficient to subdue an adversary. In one instant he becomes a murderer, a sociopath, even though he may be protected by the law or by a badge. Similarly, dogs occasionally lose their control of inhibition, and threat becomes an attack. My three-year-old son was playing too close to the dog's feed bowl the other day. I warned him to keep away as the dog growled. He heeded neither my warning nor the dog's. Suddenly the dog turned and snapped at his face. The bite was inhibited, and the boy was merely frightened. It was a good lesson. But sometimes a dog's bite is not inhibited. I am forced to the conclusion that such dogs, a product of domestication and possibly of improper rearing, have no bite inhibition and in a sense are sociopaths. Other cases of dogs attacking people without any apparent control often occur when a person insists on approaching a strange dog without reading its intention or without giving the dog a chance to read his.

There have been many reports of the incredible heroism and loyalty of certain dogs. They defend the home against intruders, warn the owners of danger such as fire or rescue a drowning child. Are such actions purely instinctual, or are they at some higher altruistic level? I am inclined to think it is most certainly the latter. What I have found in the wolf is that the individual has a great allegiance to the pack, and in the domesticated dog his pack companions are human beings. This relationship is the consequence of early socialization. Therefore, I regard the cases of heroism and loyalty as not really so fantastic as they are thought to be. Such actions are within the natural capacities of dogs and wolves. The dog's pack consists mainly of human beings, and to them he will show the same deep allegiance as one wolf will for his wolf pack companions.

With this pack identity, the individual wolf cooperates with others for the benefit of the group, as in hunting and in defending territory. There is a great community spirit expressed by all as they engage in choral howling and in ceremonial displays of affection to the leader and to each other. Also, males never attack females, and the male assists his mate to excavate the den and to feed the cubs. Other pack members—an "aunt" or an "uncle"—may also tend the cubs or baby-sit while the parents take a break. And, of course, the male never attacks and kills the offspring.

We can say the same things about domesticated dogs, but there are exceptions: Male *will* attack female. He may show no interest in his offspring and may even attack them, especially if he is jealous. If the owner is threatened or in danger, some companion dogs will rally to his assistance just as the wolves will suddenly behave as one coordinated and united pack. A kind of single-mindedness or collective consciousness of the group, not the uniform hysteria of a mob, seems to emerge. Other dogs will stand and observe, or flee. Such behavior is reminiscent of the "bystander apathy" of city crowds that watch some atrocity but do not lift a finger to assist. Certainly some of this may be due to fear, which is excusable in man or dog, but the apathy is a sign of some deeper social sickness.

We all wonder how our dogs might react if we were in some kind of trouble. You might fake a scene: A friend comes over and pretends to attack you and your dog comes running over wagging his tail, just sits with a puzzled expression on his face or walks off and ignores you. You are disappointed. But this is hardly a fair test, for your dog can read the silent language that you were unable to fake to convince him that you were in trouble. Dogs have to be trained to attack, and many fail the course not because they are timid but because they are well socialized to people and, like wolves, have a tremendous built-in inhibition about inflicting physical injury on their human pack companions. Some breeds, though, are much easier to train than others for attack and guard work, so there may be genetic factors operating. Or are there? Many such dogs fail the course because the trainer cannot break down the dogs' natural inhibitions against attacking.

It is another question why these biological and cultural inhibitions break down in man. There are many factors that can turn man against man, that can make man commit genocide or massacre unarmed people. Something seems to click, and the trained dog or soldier appears to act automatically, as though the adversary were an object, a different being, an alien. Such instant breaking of the social bond, the allegiance for fellow man, enables one to attack and to kill even one's brother, when one's distorted (and trained-indoctrinated) mind perceives him as an alien (because he has different beliefs or is of a different culture or color). There are recorded cases of faithful dogs suddenly attacking their owners when the owner accidentally falls, for example. In that split second, the dog may not recognize the owner struggling on his back, and he either backs off fearfully or attacks defensively. Occasionally dogs roaming in the woods have killed children. Perhaps the children were rolling around and were for one fatal moment not quite human. Or perhaps the dogs, like human hunters, were trigger happy. They were tuned to respond to the slightest movements in the cover and attacked automatically. This is one reason, perhaps, why hunter has shot fellow hunter or cow or even child on a bicycle. We excuse his actions, but few will excuse the dog, who is instantly branded a killer. As a dog that has "reverted" to its wild instinctual state, even though he is loyal and trustworthy at home, few owners and no neighbors would allow such an animal to live. But dog, like man, will react automatically or instinctively under certain circumstances, in this case not savagely or murderously, but purely to kill efficiently as a hunter in response to a moving object. It is an accident of nature, an accident for which we find it easier to excuse and forgive the hunter than the dog, although both may be equally innocent.

I have heard occasionally of dogs biting their owners or other people for no apparent reason. When we dig into these incidents, two things often come up. First, the owners have been too lenient, too permissive with the dog during its infancy. With such lack of discipline, some dogs remain perpetual puppies, enjoying their owners' indulgence, but others as they mature attempt to become the dominant (leader wolf) of the household. And some succeed. Such rivalry and testing of the owners for social status is really quite normal. In any group—wolf, dog or human—one individual will be a leader, and if there is no clear leadership, some fighting or conflict breaks out until one is established. Then a kind of pecking order or social hierarchy exists which brings peace through order. Each individual knows his or her place, and there is no further conflict or fighting. An individual that has not learned his place is socially maladjusted; he has no respect for authority or social order and shows no mercy for subordinates. These abnormalities, coupled with a lack of social conscience and morality in both dog and human being, are principally a consequence of early rearing experiences: The parents of either pup or child clearly have a tremendous responsibility.

In the wolf pack, the cubs soon learn their place and manners—not to be too obtrusive to their parents or to a grumpy old uncle. Just as in man, there is also clear evidence of kinship, for the offspring of socially high-ranking parents have a higher social status than the young of lower-ranking individuals.

Social competition for status is perhaps one of the sicker aspects of modern Western society, when the individual tends to function not for the welfare of the group but purely in his own selfish interests. Such a wolf would not live long. When man gets frustrated with unsuccessful attempts to seek status and recognition, he may vent his frustration on innocent subordinates and even on his wife and family. We see the same redirection of aggression toward subordinates in many animals, including dogs and farmyard chickens.

We have learned one more thing from wolves and other wild dogs that is perhaps a lesson, a red light of warning to man. They do not overkill; they never pick out the prize animal of the herd, like the perverted white trophy hunter who attempts and unfortunately too often succeeds in doing. The wolf pack has an almost mystic or cosmic relationship with its prey—be it caribou, deer or Dall sheep. Only the weakest, the oldest and the sickest are killed off, and this kind of pruning knife effect is of immense value to the herd, for otherwise they might multiply too fast and eat themselves out of all available food in one or two generations. The wolf pack serves an invaluable purpose in regulating their numbers and in controlling the quality of the herd. The most remarkable thing, though, is the fact that even in times of plenty, the wolf pack does not increase in size, nor does it overkill. Through very complex social birth control mechanisms, the pack maintains the same size year after year.

Now compare this perfect ecological balance of nature with the chaos that man can create. He destroys the wolf packs and then finds the deer are multiplying too fast and hundreds are slowly starving. So the park services have to move in and kill off an estimated number each year that are even in excess of the hunters' bag during the shooting season.

Unlike the wolf, who is, unless man interferes, at one with his environment, man has gained greater and greater control over his environment, and as a consequence all the natural methods that control the human population, such as disease, starvation, infertility and infant mortality, no longer operate. Man has been slow to realize that he is not omnipotent and free and that he must now develop some new means of controlling his population growth. "Freedom" must be regulated. His greatest danger is that he will destroy himself not through war but through overpopulation, the pressure> of which is already affecting our lives in many ways. We have polluted the earth, air and water, and our cities are surrounded by the excrement of our progress. We have voraciously overkilled, and our natural resources are being depleted at an alarming rate. Crowding stress, breakdown of moral codes and of human dignity, the identity crisis—all these problems emerge as we develop an increasingly complex society. We might dream of life as it was once in the tribe, where, as in the wolf pack, each individual knew his place, each contributed to the welfare of the group, and each had the dignity and security of self-identity and group-identity. There was fellowship, allegiance, community spirit and an internal strength that came from such a unity of families.

Many people agree that the study of wolves and other animal societies and of the few remaining tribes (as yet uncontaminated by our technologically overdeveloped and culturally undeveloped civilization) may lead us to a deeper understanding of the phenomenon of man. But before this we need action programs to improve the quality of life and to prevent further contamination and depletion of the biosphere.

Some say that dogs could never have evolved from wolves because wolves are so aggressive toward dogs that intrude upon their territory. Certainly domestication has had a great influence on canine behavior, much in the same way as cultural evolution has affected our own behavior. The average pet dog has transferred his pack allegiance and identity to the human family with whom he now lives, and the territory that he defends is their home and property. It is indeed a very compatible relationship. On neutral territory, such as in the neighborhood park, dogs and people are friendly and can enjoy each other's company without having to defend either territory or status. But both dog and man will retaliate even in the park if that crucial personal sphere is violated. An adult dog or human being normally tolerates intrusions into the personal sphere if the intruder is an infant, a clearly subordinate individual or an attractive member of the opposite sex. But a person from another culture, or a breed of dog with a very different personal distance, may intrude on and offend the other. Friendly intentions may be misinterpreted, and such misreading may lead to mutual avoidance or even to fighting. This is something that man is at last beginning to comprehend. Perhaps future peace treaty discussions and other international confrontations on some neutral territory may progress more smoothly and have a more fruitful outcome when both parties understand and respect each other's cultural differences. For beneath these differences are the mutually shared feelings and qualities of human beings who desire peace and unity but are afraid and defensive when faced with others whom they do not understand and with whom they cannot fully communicate.

It is almost like two dogs in opposite yards that are never allowed to get to know each other on neutral territory or to become socialized. They constantly growl and threaten each other, each defending his territorial rights, and neither dog can reach the other because of the fence between them. The fence between nations is a double one consisting of a mutual suspicion and fears of annihilation and a mutual misreading, the inability to communicate through the invisible cultural barrier. Our dogs might get along well, not if we suddenly remove the fence, but if we take them into the park, away from the territories that they feel impelled to defend habitually in their daily displays of aggression. If we then take them home and the fence is removed while they are away, would they not become friends? (Or would they form an alliance and threaten the next dog on the block behind its owner's fence?) I realize that making such analogies between the suburban dog's life and international diplomacy is a long shot, but the basic principles operating are surprisingly similar. The social life and morality of wolves and wild dogs in nature and of the domesticated dog adapted to the social lives of its owners provide us with a wealth of information. This knowledge gives us not only a deeper insight into our own nature but also into the ways in which our cultural standards and ethical and moral codes can affect others. To accept the fact that animals have certain codes and standards is a beginning, a loosening up of our self-centered or ethnocentric outlook. We may then begin to understand and communicate at a meaningful level once the barriers of culture, fear and distrust are broken down. It is often hard to realize that the dog on the other side of the fence has the same emotions, hopes and suspicions and is a member of the same species, when his appearance is so very different in terms of size, color or some other distinguishing feature that makes him appear alien in form and behavior.

In comparing and contrasting the morality of dogs and men, the possibility emerges that while man faces certain problems in becoming civilized, so the dog, with a number of wild characteristics and instincts not completely eliminated by selective breeding, faces certain perplexing problems in becoming domesticated.

11

Some Problems of Domestication— for Man and Dog

FEW OF US are really 100 percent happy with our lot. There's something perpetually just out of reach, a promise of eternal sunset over the next hill, and the grass is always greener on the other side of the fence. Every man, or Everyman, faces countless frustrations, many of which are enforced culturally by the way in which he was raised and by the culture in which he now lives. He must conform to certain social codes, even if deep down he doesn't believe in them or even if they were opposed to the basic desires and drives of human nature. It was Freud's genius that first recognized how many of the emotional problems of mankind stem from early rearing and from the frustration of man's basic instincts by various social repressions.

Man emerging into a technological world is forced to cooperate with others, on whom he becomes dependent. Society is as much responsible to the individual as the individual is to society. He can no longer behave as a free individual within a close-knit family unit or clan. He must acquire a social conscience—the superego—and he, as a species, is now evolving along an almost impossible path, where he must maintain and develop his own individuality, preserve his personal identity, and yet become part of the "collective consciousness" of the masses which form his own particular culture. It is a dynamic process of development, change, shifts in values and goals from one generation to the next. We call it civilization, in which man evolves from a diversity of cultures, which share similarities and

169

contain subtle differences in degrees of freedom of the individual's natural basic drives, tolerance for idiosyncrasy and personal taste, differences in esthetic appreciation and materialistic values, and so on.

Changes can be so rapid in a dynamically evolving, complex technological society that the individual may find it difficult to adapt. This stress, the stress of constantly adapting and readapting to change, has been called "future shock" in a book of the same title by Alvin Toffler. We are at this stage now, and it may get worse. But future shock is only one of the problems that modern man (and, as we will see, his dog) has to face. He is exposed to crowding stress—the exhausting denervation of a high frequency of social interaction. This may be compensated partially by putting on blinkers or filters and simply engaging in impersonal superficial transactions with his fellows. But this may lead to feelings of loneliness, of dehumanization, aggravated by the sense of being depersonalized by the complex, anonymous social machinery of corporate empires. The architecture and layout of many of our cities are no help either. Designed for cars and commuters, they include no places for people to sit, walk and interact with each other.

There is so much information and event in the world nowadays that the human brain experiences overload—another stress. Some people who are successful and are in great demand become overcommitted and, spreading themselves too thin, they grow ineffectual, or else they rise up the status hierarchy and in accordance with the "Peter Principle" become impotent executives. Many young people suffer from diffuse anxieties and identity crises (where am I, what am I, where am I going—and who cares), new social sicknesses related to the apparent anonymity and materialistic values of our technological society. Relations between husband and wife are stressed because while one is frustrated and overworked, the other, the wife, may be frustrated, repressed and bored. Both partners rely more and more on each other and make increasing demands on each other to compensate for the inadequacies of their lives, and this puts further pressure on the marriage bond. Indeed the entire institution of marriage is changing and reflects some of the real problems people have in effectively communicating their needs and in understanding each other. The increase in sensitivity training and group therapy sessions shows how stressed and disordered our lives and relationships with each other can be. Some people adapt in one way or another by developing a hobby or other creative and rewarding activity. Others overcompensate in their work and become compulsive, success-oriented status seekers, finding personal emptiness when they attain their goal. Many compensate by game playing, assuming some role behind which they can hide themselves, only to find again that life is an empty façade. Anxieties may be temporarily alleviated by acquisitive greed, by collecting money or expensive consumer goods, but this, too, is no solution and does not satisfy the basic human needs for love, self-esteem, creative freedom and self-fulfillment. We might wonder, then, if the canine companion of Western man is ever affected by future shock and some of the other poignant stresses of modern society.

Wherever man is, somewhere in his culture we find the dog, in a particular place, fulfilling certain functions that each culture has allotted man's closest companion. In one culture the dog may be purely utilitarian and a vital part of the economy. An Eskimo without dogs to pull his sled and to smell out seals from their breathing holes would be lost. He is totally dependent on his dogs and much of his life and culture revolves around the dog—and the seal. In other cultures, the dog is used exclusively for herding cattle or sheep, or for hunting, for coursing game in the desert, or he is kept as a food item that until eaten is a nice companion for the children to play with and to keep down the vermin in the village. A more general use of dogs common to many cultures is that of a companion and guard. Now in the very diverse culture developed by modern Western man we find the dog in the many diverse roles enumerated above (with the exception of the food role), and there are many different breeds now more or less standardized. Most can be classified according to their utility function: terriers, bird dogs, trail or scent hounds, coursing hounds, guard dogs, etc. In some cases we find that the dog reflects the human culture that developed it; thus an agrarian or farming culture developed guarding and herding dogs, hunting communities developed hunting dogs especially fitted to the terrain and kind of animal that was hunted.

These traits have been preserved in many breeds from the Middle Ages, when only the landed gentry used dogs for pleasure, until now, when Everyman can enjoy his sporting or working dog, be it for sled-racing competitions, sheepherding or a gundog trial—or for treeing coons. The service provided by such dogs is really nonessential to the economic survival of Western man, in sharp contrast to other cultures that were once or still are very much dependent on the working dog. In the complex culture in which we now live, working dogs still work, of course, as farm dogs, herders, guards and hunters, but only a small segment of people really need the dog in the economic sense. The modern working dogs now fill new roles as social or club cards. Their basic instincts, which have been brought out through selective breeding and are still of value to the owner, remain unchanged. This point should be borne in mind for later discussion, where it will be seen that some of these natural tendencies and basic instincts of the modern domesticated dog which are difficult to inhibit can be very undesirable under the restricted conditions of urban life.

A few new tasks for working dogs have evolved in our Western culture, such as guiding the blind and mine detecting for the Army. Again, utilizing basic traits and instinctual patterns of suitable breeds made accessible by selective breeding, Western man continues to evolve specialist dogs for selected jobs.

A new slot for the dog is afforded in all cultures that have some degree of affluence. It is only then that we can indulge ourselves with dogs "for their own sake" and consequently indulge our dogs as household pets in air-conditioned, centrally heated, vermin-free abodes, where food for man and beast comes in cans or plastic wrappers, hygienically prepared and preserved and nutritionally balanced with appropriate additives. The Egyptian, Greek and Chinese civilizations indulged themselves in breeding fine nonworking companion dogs that had esthetically pleasing or emotionally satisfying behavioral traits and physical characteristics. They, like their owners, were nonworking aristocrats. These dogs reflected their owners socially, in terms of status, for few could afford to possess such canine luxuries. Their emergence through domestication and careful selective breeding also reflected the evolution of the human culture that developed them.

Western civilization, compared to these earlier cultures, is per capita the most affluent in the history of mankind and unique in terms of a large and wealthy middle class. In the previous civilizations, there were kings and aristocrats with pet dogs and peasants with working dogs. A peasant's dog had to earn its keep, for few could afford to feed an extra noncontributing mouth, and a man was very probably socially inhibited from owning a dog above his station.

Now on the verge of the twenty-first century the scene is very different. We find urban and suburban man still with his dog. As man's role in society has changed, so has his dog's; no longer are they hunters or herders. We find old breeds in new roles and working dogs that no longer work. Some are now companions or ornaments, or child-substitutes, or status symbols, or else they fulfill other desires of their owners, be it for strength, agility, beauty or aggression: Dogs are of therapeutic value. Man is supposedly a very adaptive animal, and some say he can adjust to almost any kind of existence. But some of us are beginning to question this, for life is now so complex, and daily frustrations together with the stressful conditions of urban life greet the commuter from the dormitory suburbs—the stresses of pollution, overcrowding and inadequate roads and buildings discussed earlier. With all this it is easy to forget that around the corner is pain and poverty in the ghettos, of which we are reminded only when there is violence. We are not really complacent—we are confused, stressed and frustrated. We are being forced to adapt to an almost pathological state. So release and relaxation through vacations, home life, the dog and related dog clubs, acquisition of material things and escape for some through television, alcohol or drugs are socially acceptable—

acceptable, because man needs a break from the tedium of routine work, from intense creativity, from stressful competition. It is a rare man who does not èxperience any frustration, and he is not necessarily a happy man. A happy man is one who has earned the freedom and respect to be able to "do his own thing."

When a man has few alternatives, little choice in being able to realize his ambitions—be they for equal opportunity, creative and intellectual freedom or for a better standard of living and fair income—he experiences increasing frustration. As more doors are closed in his face or are never discovered, he comes to believe he has little to live for and nothing to lose by resorting to crime and violence. On the one hand his superego, his social conscience, has not developed because of his impoverished rearing and lack of contact with the affluent majority who determine the social and cultural norm. On the other hand, his basic needs and desires may be so frustrated and repressed by society that he is literally a prisoner—like a hunting dog cooped up in his suburban backyard with nothing to chase and "kill" or retrieve except the mailman and his own tail.

Against the background of man's dilemmas, I now want to focus on the dog that he has brought with him into this new life-style. How much does the dog share with his master in terms of frustration of his basic urges, and how well is the dog adapted to his master's present life-style, both genetically and through training and by the provision of substitute outlets?

Like his suburban or urban owner, the dog has to conform to many restrictions, and what is biologically normal for a dog (or master) to do is often not socially acceptable. Also, like his owner, there may be few outlets or alternatives for many natural tendencies and basic instincts, so that they may build up inside. Frustration is then experienced and the pent-up drive may be discharged out of the blue by the most inappropriate stimuli and under the most unexpected circumstances. Or frustration may lead to aggression. Another thing may happen, which Dr. H. Hediger, director of the Zurich Zoo, described in zoo animals—namely, a hypertrophy or overmagnification of values. The dog, as well as his owner, becomes overcovetous and overdefensive of certain possessions or of his territory or companion. Another problem that faces people and dogs is that they are supposed to be civil if not friendly to strangers, and the dog especially is expected to accept people and behave in a gentle way (unless he is a guard dog). For the average house pet this can be a problem, and we will look into the genetics and rearing conditions that seem to influence this "oversocial behavior" of our modern dog. A few examples will illustrate these points. Many dogs have a pretty miserable sex life; they have been selectively bred so that they reach sexual maturity at an early age and are also promiscuous, for refusal to mate with certain individuals would not help any breeding program. Against this background, which man has produced in the dog, the average dog leads a life of chastity. He meets a neighboring bitch and she has been spayed or already bred to a stud several hundred miles away. Or even worse, he smells that she is in heat, but the owners keep her confined until her period of sexual receptivity is over. What would the average all-American male do under such circumstances? Sexual frustration is one common cause of violence in man, and certainly it is not unusual in dogs. Some dogs, because they are raised more or less exclusively with human beings, may become oversocialized to people. When they reach sexual maturity they may really yearn for their masters and ignore or repel other dogs. Often such "people dogs" are difficult to handle when they are in heat, as are male people dogs that get "turned on" when being petted by someone, especially if that person is carrying the odor of a dog that is in heat. Imagine the frustration and confusion! One solution is to spay or castrate the dog. Sexual frustrations in man have many more alternatives, such as vicariously enjoying a "flesh film," driving one's car fast and furiously, or engaging in exhausting physical activity; making the boys take long cross-country runs is a popular practice in English boarding schools, perhaps better than putting saltpeter in their tea!

What natural outlets does the pet dog have for hunting, tracking, stalking, biting, shaking and killing prey? We might provide him with surrogate objects, such as a piece of rawhide or a ball, but these are pale substitutes. Most of the games dogs really enjoy with their owners involve chasing and "killing," or retrieving, a suitable prey object thrown by the owner, be it a stick or a ball. But if the dog doesn't have anything or anyone to play with, what other outlets are there for this hunting instinct? Some breeds are luckier than others because their hunting instinct has been more or less bred out of them. But others, especially the terriers and hunting dogs that are kept as house pets with no "work" to do, have a hard time. So they seek substitute objects that are not always socially acceptable. The moving legs of a passerby or the wheels of a bicycle or car become substitute "releasing stimuli" for prey chasing. This is also one reason why dogs like to chase cats. A good reciprocal arrangement has been set up between these two species under the restrictions of domesticity, the cat satisfying the needs of the dog to chase something and perhaps to a lesser degree the dog triggering the cat to satisfy flight reactions. A young wolf or coyote responds instinctively to reasonably small, receding, moving objects: This is part of the reflexlike hunting behavior. And so the dog, having chased the "prey," has to bite and kill it. Thus the mailman is so often bitten as he is *leaving* the garden, or the child running past the house gets a bad nip on the ankle. Is the dog in question savage? Should he be destroyed? In fact, he is suffering from repression of his normal instincts. Such natural tendencies might be controlled through punishment, but that would only bottle things up more. I remember living in a semirural area and my nonworking sheep dog really needed to work. His herding instincts got badly frustrated. So he would often escape and run off for the day, going from one farm to the next to bark at and herd up all the cattle and sheep. Again, like the dog using the receding mailman's trousers as a prey substitute, my sheep dog found an appropriate outlet for his need to herd and chase by going the rounds through the meadows. He and other dogs who often joined him were quickly branded as killers, but the real problem was the farmer's conviction that disturbed cows produce less milk!

Why do many dogs like to break out occasionally and go off and roll in the most nauseating materials and scavenge all kinds of unmentionable garbage when they have nice clean homes and a good balanced diet? Just like all of us wanting to break away from routine and have an eating orgy, so does the dog! His natural behavior is to roam and scavenge—really a form of work—and he probably has great fun doing the rounds of the garbage cans that contain all kinds of exciting things. One possible reason is that wearing an odor for a dog is akin to man's desire to put on new or fancy clothes. We indulge ourselves this way, so why can't our dogs indulge their senses too?

A dog is supposed to be friendly if not downright submissive and obsequious to all people who come into his home. He must accept all comers once they have been introduced, and this is a hard task for any dog in his right mind. Some people are too noisy, smelly, overindulgent and want the dog to do all kinds of uncanine things. With a large dog such as a Malemute, okay, people will accept his aloofness and say he is a proud animal who only shows affection when he feels like it. But so many dogs that I have met shower me with excessive and unsolicited affection. They seem oversociable and submissive, yet with other dogs they will stand their ground and often assert their dominance. One explanation for this behavior is that in domesticating dogs we have selected for certain infantile behaviors, especially submission and attention-seeking. This notion is supported by Dr. Erik Zimen's studies of dogs and wolves in Kiel, West Germany. He finds that a number of these behaviors disappear from the wolf's repertoire as he matures, but in dogs they may persist indefinitely. So many dogs behave submissively toward all people. They regard them as their social superiors and this does have advantages, for it makes the dog more reliable as a pet. People can approach and make contact with him with equanimity. But it has a drawback, too, for all dogs are not like this. Some are like their wolf ancestors, having a close allegiance to their human family or pack and being wary of strangers. People get the idea that all dogs are friendly and they may presume too much on one of these individuals and suffer the consequences of a growl, an inhibited bite or even worse if they persist!

A dog will defend its offspring against strangers, and this natural behavior can be a problem. I have heard of dogs that are so protective of their master's children that it is dangerous for strangers to forcibly intrude. Often the neighbor's children may be driven off. But some dogs do make remarkable fostermothers, and none of these "social problems" ever arise.

A dog has a need for privacy, someplace to call his own den, and his need to maintain some degree of social distance should be respected. He needs somewhere to retire, to escape from children and perhaps a place where he can rest and contemplate. These natural needs should be respected and provided for.

One real biological problem for the domesticated bitch is that if she isn't mated, she will often become pseudopregnant. Toward the end of the "pregnancy" she may start to produce milk, make a nest, and take a slipper or even a leash as a substitute puppy which she guards faithfully. Imagine a series of consecutive false pregnancies, each one a pathetic letdown, where maternal behavior is turned on and can only be released through some phantom puppy object. We do know that wild canids experience false pregnancies, but usually they are ultimately mated and have young. If they do have a pseudopregnancy, it may not go any farther than a slight enlargement of the nipples. Possibly as a result of man's hand in domesticating dogs, he has influenced the hormonal system so much that pseudopregnancy, pseudolabor and pseudonursing behavior can and does occur in many dogs. We should spay bitches or breed them to prevent this behaviorally and hormonally disturbing phenomenon from repeatedly occurring.

Dogs have adapted extremely well to our present way of life, perhaps even better than Western man himself, but both man and dog do experience a number of social restrictions and limitations imposed by living in an urban or suburban environment where there are few appropriate stimuli to release or satisfy basic needs. We are only beginning to understand some of the limitations in the environment which we have so drastically and shortsightedly imposed on ourselves. Some of us break out and seek a simpler and more satisfying life in the country, but most of us are forced for economic reasons into behaviorally inadequate urban and suburban environments. A few people break off and form a commune, a subculture within the existing structure. Alan Beck, working for his PhD at Johns Hopkins University, is studying urban dog packs. Dogs, too, can break off and some become feral while others spend time out with the pack and time at home. I wonder if he will find neighboring dog packs engaging in dog fights like the teen-age gangs in some of our cities!

One final analogy. Under intensive, crowded living, an animal becomes more suspicious and defensive, if not almost paranoid, about the safety of his territory and property. These fears are increased when there is competition and even theft. So it is with man, who becomes more covetous of his house and possessions if he has had to work hard and compete for them and when theft and vandalism are widespread. When his living space is crowded in by a large populace, crowding stress also increases his need to withdraw into his own shell, and consequently the importance of his little plot and the basic need to protect it increases. In many neighborhoods, dogs, like people, are friendly when they are out together in a pack or crowd on neutral territory, but on their home ground strangers are treated with suspicion and are often unwelcome. In areas where there are many dogs and people, the dog has to work hard to maintain his territory, so he barks a lot, stakes out his territory daily with urine marks and puts on an aggressive front when strange dogs or people enter his little plot. These behaviors related to territoriality are certainly magnified, as is the case in man, under crowded conditions. To this we should add the fact that many dogs were originally selected to be good guards at a time when there was far less crowding.

The dog is exposed to many of the social problems that confront his master, including crowding stress and the restrictions and frustrations of imprisonment in suburbia's gilded ghettos. The bored housewife shares the same bland routine as does her dog; both may grow fat and spend much of the day asleep in front of the television, or both may erupt under the pressures of understimulation. Similarly, the harrassed, high-strung mother may need tranquilizers to get through the day to stall off a nervous breakdown; it is more than one pet dog that can't take the frenetic pace of such households and becomes a nervous wreck, hiding under the table when the children come home from school or biting them through fear and confusion. Even the executive, struggling to maintain his status in a highly competitive world, is in some ways like his dog, who in a suburb full of dogs has to preserve his identity and status by marking and defending his territory against rival neighbors. Man also defends his conceptual territory, his world of ideas and personal beliefs, much in the same way as an animal will defend his physical territory, and stress and anxiety can result when this territory is threatened or challenged by others.

I have drawn some analogies, some of which are not so far out, between dog and human behavior in relation to some of the problems of everyday life. Fortunately there are fewer canine sociopaths than there are human, and it is quite possible that the dog is adapting better than his master to the way of life that we have created for ourselves.

12

Socially and Emotionally Maladjusted Dogs: Canine Delinquents and Sociopaths

A FEW YEARS ago it was the "in" thing to rear children permissively, giving them total freedom and only disciplining them when their lives were in danger. The repercussions of such rearing practice are varied and range in extremes. Some indulged children grew up to become well-adjusted adults, while others had the greatest difficulty in handling the transition from childhood dependency to adult independence. Some found it difficult to accept responsibility after years of irresponsible growth where every whim and fancy was catered to. Some children, perhaps, had a sheltered life, their overprotective parents either not allowing or not fostering peer interaction and socialization, an essential part of growing up where the child socializes with peers of different ages outside the classroom.

Certainly the Victorian approach—rearing children in an atmosphere of discipline and repression, where they are to be seen and not heard and not allowed to speak until spoken to—is just as deplorable. Children are rebellious, especially at around three years of age and later in adolescence, and this rebelliousness is associated with the development of the child's individuality and independence. The child has to learn to handle his fears and frustrations that bring out aggression, has to learn the ethics and moral codes of his culture and has to sort out his own convictions, conscience and sense of responsibility and identity.

But wait— Isn't this chapter supposed to be about dogs,

181

you're thinking. The truth is the developmental patterns that pups and children go through are very similar, and the different methods of rearing often have analogous effects on both man and dog.

To begin with, we should make a distinction between those species that can be easily and permanently socialized to man and other species that cannot and possibly identify why this is so. Several species of animals—dogs, cats, pigs, sheep and horses— if they are handled early in life will become attached to people. Dogs, elephants and horses seem generally to maintain a closer attachment than other domesticated species because in nature they respond to a leader in the pack or herd. The owner represents a substitute leader, and for a dog, as I mentioned previously, other people in the household may represent members of his pack. Less gregarious species, such as cats, raccoons and ocelots, live a more solitary life in nature and do not respond to a leader figure, nor do they always accept discipline. During early life when they normally have a loose attachment to their parents they will make good pets because the owner is essentially a parent surrogate. But as they mature they are becoming more and more independent, less subordinate and more difficult to train, discipline or even to indulge with affection and close contact. Many young animals (and people) are quite difficult to handle when they first reach sexual maturity. This adolescent phase is the beginning of independence from parental care, discipline and domination. In nature, this phase results in the offspring of some species—coyotes and jackals are a good example—leaving the parents. In other animals, separation from the parents occurs well before sexual maturity. Increasing intolerance of parents toward young and their eventual abandonment is seen in the red fox, for example. And littermates become increasingly intolerant of each other and ultimately go their separate ways. Wolves are somewhat different because, unlike foxes or coyotes, they do not split up at some set age but instead they come together as a pack. Bonds formed early in life are more or less permanent. Some rivalry over mates occurs during the breeding season, but preferences, pair bonds and allegiances tend to reduce conflicts. Perhaps the greatest social stabilizer is the existence of a clear dominance hierarchy. Of course the social order *does* change over the years, but the hierarchical system serves to promote peace and order. To this we should add the fact that wolves seem to have a need to belong to the pack, to display their allegiance to their superiors in ceremonial patterns of greeting and obeisance.

These differences and subtleties of social behavior in the wild relatives of domesticated dogs give us some insight into how the natural disposition and propensities of our dogs accord with the ways in which we keep them. We may also recognize some of the wrong ways to raise our dogs, ways that may not be in harmony with their natural tendencies or that may bring out the worst in our pets and make them socially maladjusted delinquents.

Another point to consider is the competition (analogous to sibling rivalry in children) of other dogs for the affection of a newly acquired pup. A "resident" adult dog may resent the addition of a new pup to the home and display his jealousy in various ways, ranging from sulking and not eating his food to actually attacking the pup and punishing it when the owners are not around. But, on the other hand, the resident dog may accept the pup and spend a good deal of time with him, so that the pup may become too attached to the dog and not closely bonded to its owners as usually occurs when he is the only dog in the family. Overattachment to another dog, which may make the pup less attached and dependent on owners, may also make the pup less trainable. This has been shown by J. P. Scott, B. E. Ginsberg and C. J. Pfaffenberger in their studies of various rearing procedures of potential guide dogs for the blind. A pup raised, say, with its mother or a littermate for the first twelve weeks, even if it has had plenty of human contact, will generally be an inferior candidate for training to one that has been raised almost exclusively with people from six or eight weeks of age.

Equate this with the kibbutz system of raising children on the Israeli farm communes. The children are exposed to constant interaction. This is clearly of high priority, for socialization with the peer group will facilitate later social interaction with individuals of the same generation. Interaction with parents is not exclusive: The children are also exposed to many adults and to children of widely differing ages. They do not become exclusively socialized to one age group or just to their parents, and adverse parental influences are diluted. Contrast this with the Western pattern of child-rearing, especially the "only (spoiled) child," where, as in the case of many dogs, children become overattached to their parents. Add to this the notion of some school boards that plan to break down local neighborhood schools, not primarily into integrated schools but into integrated schools specialized for one or two grades only. Imagine your child surrounded exclusively at school by peers of the same age. He would have no older peers to emulate or younger children to show off to.

Many parents treat their children or their pets like objects or vegetables, attending only to their basic needs. Child or pup in such a situation may experience little love or affection. Or he may receive plenty of affection, this not being the main issue. The main issue is that the child or pup is *not* exposed to a rich and varied environment, and such exposure as shown in Chapter 6 is vital for normal development. The child is kept in the house of affluent monotony with a television for company, the pup in the backyard with nothing to do except bark and play with a ball. Child or pup is taken out in the car occasionally and is rarely allowed out alone.* The outside world is to be seen but not touched, rarely smelled or tasted and never explored or manipulated. This is a kind of experiential deprivation which is both subtle and insidious but which may severely limit development and the realization of latent potentials. A laboratory experiment with cats conducted by Drs. R. Held and A. Hein a few years ago demonstrated that a cat having the same visual experiences as its laboratory partner but no opportunity to explore grows up into an inferior individual, deficient in many abilities that its partner has been able to develop.

*In some places, notably Chicago, it is a criminal offense to take a dog into the park. Who would have believed this fifty years ago, before the population explosion of dogs and people, that parks would be closed to defecating dogs!

A variety of behavioral disorders may also develop as a consequence of one of two extremes of rearing—namely, overpermissive (indulgent) or disciplinary rearing. Dr. D. G. Freedman, while at the Jackson Laboratory at Bar Harbor, Maine, experimentally raised beagles, Shetland sheep dogs, wirehaired fox terriers and basenjis under these opposite conditions. When disciplined at a later age not to eat from a food pan when the experimenter left the room, both indulged and disciplined groups of Shetland sheep dogs did not eat, while both groups of basenjis ate, the basenjis being more outgoing and less timid than the shelties. Permissively raised beagles and wirehaired fox terriers did not eat when the experimenter left the room, while those that had been raised with prior disciplinary training did. Clearly we can make no generalizations as to how one rearing practice or another can influence later trainability; we must know something about the inherited temperament characteristics of the breed or particular strain, be it timid, strong-willed, shy or outgoing, in order to make some predictions as to how a particular rearing method will influence later behavior, etc.

There are also some other intriguing consequences of this experiment. Overindulged beagles became extremely shy with the experimenter while indulged shelties were socially dominant over littermates that had experienced early disciplinary training.

Owners may raise their dogs either indulgently or strictly and the outcome will depend to some extent on the emotionality or temperament of their particular dog.

A timid dog that is overindulged may become overdependent and overattached—a perpetual puppy. When the pup is separated from the owner for boarding or hospitalization, a variety of separation-depression disorders may develop. These include refusal to eat (anorexia nervosa), constipation, emotional diarrhea and general physical exhaustion. Because the animal is in a state of emotional stress, its system producing high levels of the stress-reaction hormone ACTH or adrenocorticotrophic hormone, it is more directly susceptible to disease. Also, its recovery from surgery or after treatment for some disease will be impaired. Tranquilization, gentle handling and hand-feeding can be effective in such cases, plus supportive treatment with corticosteroids and antibiotics. Whenever possible, such dogs should spend as little time as possible in the veterinary hospital, because they recover much faster at home and postsurgical complications can be greatly reduced by avoiding extended postoperative hospitalization. Such an overattached dog may even pine away—literally die of starvation—as a consequence of severe depression (mourning sickness) brought on by the death of its master.

An obstacle other than separation per se that gets between such a dog and its owner may trigger an adverse reaction. He may become extremely jealous and aggressive toward a dog or person, for example, who may be visiting or toward his master's new bride (or vice versa). Sibling rivalry is another trial. The advent of a child in the family where such a dog was previously the center of attention and affection can give rise to a variety of neuroses and conversion hysterias. These include anorexia nervosa, compulsive eating, hysterical paralysis, epilepticlike convulsions and asthmalike bronchospasms.

Occasionally the overindulged dog may develop sympathy lameness. Although it is perfectly capable of using a leg that was previously injured and received veterinary treatment, it may persist in theatrical limping in the presence of its owners to ensure sympathetic attention.

In many instances the permissively raised dog may begin to take advantage of its owner—just like a teen-ager who can twist one or both parents around his little finger. The disobedient, socially maladjusted dog has the run of the house, may threaten and attack visitors and even bite its owners. The owners should be "pack leaders" and the dog affectionately subordinated. When necessary the pet should be disciplined consistently by voice command and with a direct stare. Picking the pup up or, if he is too large, shaking him by the scruff of the neck are additional disciplinary measures that are often necessary and that are highly effective. Disciplining one moment and then giving in to the pup later will only confuse him. Obedience should be rewarded with verbal praise and petting. When permissively raised pups reach sexual maturity they may become even more difficult to handle, showing extreme indifference to their owners and violent aggression when disciplined or forcibly restrained. Humane destruction is the fate of many such dogs; owners who wanted to raise their pet permissively should have chosen a more submissive and sociable breed or have had it castrated early in life to reduce the chances of sex-related aggression and dominance fighting that is associated with maturity.

These unusual cases of severe emotional disturbance have been well documented and described in detail by several authors in *Abnormal Behavior in Animals* (Saunders, Philadelphia, 1968, edited by M. W. Fox). There are, of course, even in the veterinary profession, skeptics who still insist that dogs do *not* develop emotional and psychosomatic disorders except under experimental conditions such as those designed by Pavlov to produce neuroses (or conditioned emotional reactions). There would be few such skeptics, however, if more people knew something about the basic anatomy and physiology of the canine brain. It has a cortex and an emotional (limbic) system coupled with an autonomic nervous system that is very similar in organization to what is found in the human brain. Add to this the fact that some dogs by virtue of their early socialization and close attachment to people have a relationship comparable to the relationship between child and parent. We then have the *situational* possibilities, coupled with the neural-emotional capacities, for the dog to develop behavioral disorders.

I saw my first case of an emotional breakdown in a black Labrador as a veterinary student. This dog was boarded at the local veterinary hospital where I was working while the owners went off to Europe for the summer. The dog became depressed at the separation and refused to eat anything. She rapidly began to lose weight as the anorexia nervosa persisted. The veterinarian at first thought that she had a kidney or liver disorder, or perhaps an intestinal obstruction. All clinical tests proved negative, by which time the dog had deteriorated considerably.

Taking pity on the dog, the vet's wife took it out of the kennel and gave it some warm milk in her kitchen. The dog responded dramatically and within a few days was eating voraciously. More than one poet has written about dogs pining away after the death of their masters; very often the depression, which increases susceptibility to disease, is followed by an overwhelming infection that kills the dog. Children, too, suffer from depression when separated from their parents, and some hospitals have rooming-in facilities for the mothers. Veterinarians are beginning to realize that a sojourn in the hospital can actually interfere with postsurgical recovery if the dog becomes depressed, and now they get the pet back into its home environment as soon as possible.

Then there is the case of the Pekingese that suddenly developed a total paralysis of both hind legs. The owners left it at the veterinary hospital for tests, and about a half hour after they had departed the dog was up and running around his cage. Mystified, the veterinarian called the owners and they collected their miraculously recovered pet, only to return within an hour with the dog again unable to move his hind legs. The veterinarian then dug a little deeper into the case history and found that the owners had just had their first baby after several years of marriage during which time the dog essentially became their child substitute! Sudden loss of attention when the baby came into the house was too much for the dog. The treatment, which proved effective, was to place the dog with a childless couple! This sibling rivalry only rarely results in such dramatic symptoms. More often the jealous dog will start to overeat, as though to reduce his anxieties, or he may bite one of the owners or repeatedly defecate on their bed. I once gave my parents a kitten, and this proved too much for their resident Welsh terrier. He started to eat compulsively, and since he was on a more or less ad-lib dry meal diet, he soon became extremely obese!

A veterinarian friend had two bitches, one of which suddenly had an epilepticlike fit when she scolded it for bossing the other dog, who had a litter of pups. Overexcitement can cause convulsions in high-strung dogs, and a remarkable example of this psychogenic disorder comes from Dr. Ferdinand Brunner, a veterinarian in Vienna. A couple had a dachshund that used to keel over and have a seizure whenever husband and wife had a quarrel. When the couple pretended in his surgery to have an argument the seizure occurred, but when they left the room the dog immediately got up and followed them. The dog would also have a seizure when he saw a suitcase, since the wife, after an argument, would often run around and pack a suitcase, threatening to leave her husband forever!

As an intern at Cambridge University Veterinary School I encountered one canine patient that had wheezing bronchial spasms. A chronic infection was suspected, but since the dog breathed normally after a couple of days in a hospital cage, an allergy to some agent at home seemed plausible. When the owners came to see the dog, it started wheezing again as soon as it saw them. I never did find out why the dog reacted in this manner to its owners. The stress of sustained excitement per se, however, can cause a number of psychosomatic disorders in dogs, one of the commonest being severe and often bloody diarrhea. In England I treated several small terrier and toy breeds for this ailment. Within two or three days the dog may die. At first glance the disorder looks like an acute case of garbage poisoning and, of course, should be differentiated from such a possibility. Invariably the dog had experienced some kind of trauma, like losing a fight with another dog or being upset by children staying at the house. At the beginning of the hunting season, bird dogs frequently develop a similar acute, debilitating intestinal upset attributable to overexcitement.

I have also seen a variety of compulsive behavior disorders in dogs. Dogs confined in quarantine or in a breeding kennel may display compulsive stereotyped movements such as pacing, whirling and tail chasing. Others develop the compulsive vice of eating feces or chewing and swallowing gravel or sawdust; compulsive self-grooming and licking may lead to self-mutilation or to large sores that never heal. The cause of these disorders is not primarily emotional but is, in fact, a consequence of boredom and confinement and stems from frustration of the animal's activity needs.

Many of these disorders closely parallel those seen in young infants who are exposed to comparable experiences and whose immature nervous systems are to some extent analogous to those of mature dogs. Thus in terms of aggravating or causal circumstances and the symptoms that develop, several disorders of pet dogs are comparable to those described in children by pediatric psychiatrists. Here we have the foundation for research in comparative psychiatry, where the use of animal models may not only help in the research into human disorders but may also help in the understanding and prevention of behavioral-emotional disturbances in domesticated dogs.

Some problems which may arise as a consequence of inadequate or improper rearing and handling of pups during their formative early weeks have been discussed in Chapters II and VI. Symptoms of delinquency and antisocial tendencies, even sociopathic behavior, may be attributed to improper rearing and socialization in pups and children alike. The analogies presented here deserve serious consideration, for the end result of social maladjustment in both human beings and their canine companions is a reality—a reality that must be rectified by improving rearing practices and by abandoning outdated, traditional and superstitious methods.

Schema Showing Approximate Age and Major Events in Life History of the Dog

Age

6-8 weeks   Weaning. Gradual independence.

3-12 weeks   Primary socialization period—emotional attachment to mother, littermates and human beings. Toward end of this period, *dominance hierarchy* or peck order established in litter. Will bark at and show increasing fear of strangers from 8 weeks.

12-24 weeks	Secondary socialization—relationships outside family or pack nucleus are made. Learns to handle fear of strangers and of strange places. Begins to develop strong attachment for home range, and shows signs of defending it against strangers.
24-52 weeks	May show first heat or, if male, clear interest in females. May show mate preferences based upon earlier social experiences. Defends territory against strangers, and develops awareness of and possibly respect for others' territories.
52-76 weeks	Attains full maturity, both physically and temperamentally. (Catches up with earlier sexual precocity.) May show status-seeking aggression and rivalry for "alpha" position.

13

What's Better than a Dog?

ALTHOUGH THERE ARE many breeds of dog and infinite varieties of mongrels to choose from, increasing numbers of people want something more. No, a cat won't do, not even an Abyssinian, and everyone these days seems to have to have an exotic or unusual dog like an Afghan or a Puli.

Something is hitting the dog trade and it isn't just such housing regulations as "Thou shalt not cohabit with more than one dog" or "Only two-footed residents allowed—people and parakeets." This something is man's appetite, his insatiable desire to possess the exotic, the unusual or a wild soul that he has tamed. He can vicariously enjoy the strength and beauty of his pet lion, the spirit of his puma or wolf, or the status value of his ocelot or cheetah. Similar desires may be fulfilled by the ownership of a tank of piranha fish, a ten-foot boa constrictor, a raccoon, a descented skunk. Pet stores and "ranches" advertise and peddle these animals at a fantastic rate and demand and get exorbitant prices for them.

I receive many letters from people asking advice on how to raise one of these exotic animals, and from others desperate pleas for help because their pet is giving them problems as it grows up.

The real answer to the question of whether you should own one of these exotics is to be found in the historical records of man's attempt to domesticate various wild animals. He has only been successful with a few species—those that will follow a leader or that will easily herd sheep, cattle and horses, and those that will respond to man as the leader and to the human family as their own pack. The dog is the only one of this type in the family of flesh-eating mammals, or carnivores, to have been successfully domesticated. As for the cat, it has really "adopted" man, and a cat the size of a lion would be a very unreliable pet!

The crucial characteristics that a domesticated animal must possess are reliability of temperament and trainability, both of which can be selectively bred for. An animal is domesticated only after *generations* of such selection, and even after 10,000 years some dogs have to be destroyed because they too closely resemble their wild ancestors—untrainable and unreliable in the ever-changing domestic urban or suburban environment. A characteristic common to these less social species is that they solicit and tolerate very little human contact; interaction, if any, is motivated by the desire for food. A red fox may greet its owner but permit little petting and react violently when picked up. The owner should be aware of this and respect the fact that the animal is not highly social and does not enjoy either prolonged contact or restraint. It may bite suddenly and unpredictably, and many unfortunate adults and children have received extensive facial injuries from their hand-raised raccoons.

These and other less sociable animals will also react violently when they encounter some obstacle, be it a closed door or their owner's vocal commands. Obstacles are frustrating, and frustration leads directly to aggression. The raccoon may then attack its owner, the carpet, drapes or any suitable object against which he can effectively redirect his aggression.

A wild creature can be tamed but not domesticated, and companionship with such an animal can be the experience of a lifetime. But even Gavin Maxwell's otters, recalled in his book *Ring of Bright Water,* became unreliable and aggressive as they matured. And Lois Crisler's experiences of living with hand-raised wolves in the Arctic, so vividly detailed in *Arctic Wild,* were followed by tragedies after she returned with her husband and wolves to an "enclosed" life, from which some of the wolves escaped to meet unhappy ends.

Few people have success in keeping hand-raised wild animals, not only because their personality changes as they mature, but also because the conditions under which they are kept are inadequate. A small cage or a living room is no place for a wolf or a cheetah. Few of us can be like Joy Adamson who shared the lives of lions in the wilds of the Africa she celebrated in the book and movie *Born Free.* Like Lois Crisler's wolves, her animals were free to come and go in their natural habitat. But to expect such animals to behave normally when they are kept in the very unnatural habitat of suburbia is to hope for the impossible. Some people can get by in the rural scene with a fox or a raccoon who regularly visits the farm kitchen for food and who plays with the household cat or dog, but such circumstances are the pleasure of very few.

So many of us in keeping wild, exotic animals enjoy their company only briefly. They die of some obscure disease, dietary inadequacy, or have to be destroyed or given to a zoo because they become too much to handle. Some species—small birds, fish, amphibians, reptiles and rodents, for example—are very valuable as pets, being especially instructive for children and for budding naturalists. But such wild carnivores as ocelots, raccoons, wolves and foxes are another matter entirely.

There are two main drawbacks to keeping an exotic animal as a pet, even if it has been hand-reared from early infancy. The first has already been spelled out. Few of us live in the wilderness or on a farm or have sufficient enclosed acres to safely keep one of these animals: safe from intruders, hunters or innocent people who might approach the animal incorrectly; safe for the animal who may react violently—with fear or aggression—to any change in his environment, be it a strange noise, object or person that enters his personal territory.

The second drawback is that some animals—not wolves, but foxes, raccoons and ocelots, for example—are not highly sociable when they grow up. In nature they live a solitary life except during the breeding season. So they would react to people who had hand-raised them much in the same way as they would to their own species, either aggressively as a territorial or sexual rival, or sexually as a potential mate. In dogs and wolves, the pup matures and the bond that he has with his parents (or human foster parents) persists as a social one. But in the more solitary species, the parent-infant bond breaks as the young animal matures and he goes his own way. There is little or no social bond with parents or even littermates. His parents may aggressively drive him off or desert him, and fighting within the litter also triggers each youngster's departure.

Suddenly the raccoon or ocelot turns on his owner. He is no longer an infant but a fast-maturing adolescent. With increasing sexual maturity he becomes less and less reliable. There are rare exceptions in which the animal grows out of this aggression separation period, but more often the bond is permanently broken. If he is punished or disciplined he fights even harder. Castration or spaying *may* help if the operation is done early in life, but complete success is rare.

Such an animal would not be expected to react, as a dog would, to children in the home as though they were members of his pack. The children may be attacked or avoided because they are viewed as the animal's littermates in nature, rivals for territorial space.

Too often after some bad scares or unfortunate attack the inappropriate pet is offered to the local zoo, which will rarely take him because it is inundated with such offerings. The end of the story is the familiar one: The once-beloved pet, who was such a sweet and playful infant, is humanely destroyed. Some are set free in the woods, but that is a gamble, too, for they may be unable to catch food for themselves. Worse, they may still be partly attached to people and seek them out when they are really hungry, becoming sitting ducks for hunters and a hazard for picnickers, like the semisocialized bears of our national parks, which may solicit food and then swipe and bite the hand that fed them.

The moral of the story is to stick to dogs (or cats, white mice or parakeets) and to steer clear of dreams and advertisements that tempt one to own any of the wild carnivores, even if they *have* been hand-raised. It's hard to convince people that the only pet better than a dog is another dog. They may go the long, wrong way and learn from experience, but a few may find this book. A dog is a faithful companion for the lonely or aged; a watchdog for the frightened people in our crime-ridden cities and suburbs; a trusting and always willing playmate, sometimes even a reliable baby-sitter; a "second person" without whom a blind man, a shepherd, a night watchman or an infantry patrol in the jungle would be helpless and ineffectual. Above all, a dog is a dog, and knowing something about him, about his ways, his needs and how he develops, we can learn more about the world around us and about ourselves and enrich our own lives and the knowledge of our children beyond measure.

Appendix I

Behavioral Systems and Behavior Patterns in the Dog
(Modified after J. P. Scott and J. L. Fuller, 1965)

Exploratory Behavior:

Walking or running with nose to ground, sniffing (trail following), occasionally circling and weaving to pick up trail. Often vocal and wags tail.

Walking or running and pointing (visual/auditory following).

Head raised, ears erect, occasionally standing up on hind legs.

Crawling forward, ear erect, tail low (hunting, prey stalking).

Crawling forward (rooting), head swung from side to side, or circling and pivoting on hind legs—neonatal pattern.

Approaching or standing and looking toward stimulus, ears alternately erect and flattened and body alternately raised and lowered (*i.e.,* bobbing)—especially when uncertain in novel situation, showing ambivalency of exploratory behavior and defense or withdrawal.

Social-investigative Behavior:

Circling, inguinal or facial approach.

Sniffing/licking nose, face, ear.

Anal or genital approach, sniffing/licking anal and/or genital area.

Paw raising and pawing.

Nosing and sniffing urine or feces.

Allelomimetic (Group-coordinated) Behavior:

Often combined with exploratory, social-investigative, et-epimeletic (care-giving) and agonistic behavior.

Walking, running, sitting, lying, sleeping, getting up and feeding together.

Barking or howling in unison.

Epimeletic (Self-care) Behavior:
Shelter-building:
> Digging bed in dirt or suitable material, using feet and mouth.
>
> Digging enlargement of den.

Comfort-seeking (a complex of allelomimetic (group-coordinated), epimeletic (care-giving) and etepimeletic (care-soliciting) behavior):
> Lying in a heap ("piling" in young pups).
>
> Lying close together.

Grooming: Scratching self.
> Rubbing against an object.
>
> Rubbing or rolling on ground.
>
> Biting and pulling own coat.
>
> Gnawing and pulling at nonretractile claws.
>
> Shaking.
>
> Rubbing face/eyes with forepaw.
>
> Licking anogenital areas.
>
> "Scooting" to empty anal sacs.

Epimeletic Care-giving Behavior:
> Licking pups (and adults)—body and face.
>
> Licking pups—anogenital—and ingesting excrement.
>
> Pushing pups with nose and licking anogenital areas.
>
> Carrying pups to nest.
>
> Guarding pups (aggressive behavior).
>
> Retrieving pups by nose contact or by licking face and head.
>
> Whining (possibly warning).
>
> Assuming an N posture, lying on one side, or squatting on haunches and allowing pups to nurse.
>
> Vomiting food for pups.
>
> Carrying food for pups.
>
> (Allogrooming)—licking, especially face, eyes, ears, neck and shoulder in adults.

Et-epimeletic (Care-seeking) Behavior:

Crawling forward, neck extended (rooting), with or without vocalization ("mewing" in neonate). Approach especially oriented to inguinal area.

Whining.

Yelping.

Tail wagging—usually held low and wagged to the side, ears erect or flattened.

Licking face, nose, mouth.

Jumping up.

Pawing.

Agonistic Behavior (patterns associated with conflict, generally intraspecific):

Agression and Domination:

Stalking—head and tail down, ears pricked, back arched or hindquarters raised.

Chasing, pouncing and springing.

Dominant dog stands over adversary or to one side, neck arched and head and tail raised. May adopt T posture—perpendicular to adversary with head over its shoulder—and may push.

Walks around adversary stiff-legged, neck arched, head and tail raised (agonistic circling); may wag tail stiffly.

Overt attack, biting.

Specific area of attack—face or shoulder "saddle": seizes and shakes.

Piloerection.

Baring teeth (snarling), with vertical retraction of lips to display especially the incisor and canine teeth.

May turn head away from adversary (less baring of teeth and "showing eye" than in active defense), which resembles an appeasement cut-off gesture but in reality dares the other to attack.

Growling, barking, snapping teeth, gaping ("yawn" tooth display) with growl, pawing.

Pushing or slamming with shoulder or hip against side or head of adversary.

Forepaws on adversary's back; wrestling or boxing.

Mounting and attacks neck or saddle: no pelvic thrusts.

Wagging tip of tail; tail erect.

Ears erect or ears flattened against head.

Direct gaze, pupillary dialation, "shows eye."

Play-fighting contains similar but more exaggerated components; bite is inhibited.

Defense and Subordination:

Submissive approach and greeting: forepart of body lower than hind, with head and neck extended and swung from side to side, tail curled low and wagged from side to side. When closer may flex the back and swing one hip forward so as to present the inguinal region; lingual-facial greeting.

Active Defense:

Piloerection. Snarls and shows teeth (often exaggerated).

May turn head away (laterally or lowered ventrally) from adversary, bares teeth and "shows eye."

Remains standing or sitting while adversary circles or incites.

If attacked, may attack back, snaps at adversary, attacks a subordinate or even self. Yelping and growling.

Passive Defense:

Sitting, crouching, running away.

Licking lips and occasionally showing teeth.

Submissive grin—lips retracted horizontally.

Tail between legs, ears depressed, gaze directed away from adversary (may flank-gaze). Forepaw raising.

Rolls onto back, legs extended, and does not bite (saddle area of attack thus less accessible).

Lateral recumbency, hind-leg raising, anogenital exposure (a submissive infantile posture to cut off aggression or to remotivate the aggressor).

Recumbency and complete inhibition of movement (tonic immobility).

Urination.

Defecation.

Remains standing and allows dominant dog to place feet on back.

Eliminative Behavior (Often associated with territorial scent-marking behavior and social-investigative behavior):

Urination with all four legs extended, abdomen lowered (opisthotonus) and tail raised (infantile pattern).

Adult male—raise one hind leg to urinate, often where other males urinate or around its own environment after a short absence. Rarely squats to urinate.

Adult female—urinates in squatting position, rarely raises hind leg.

Both sexes—defecation and urination in places previously used; wandering and circling, nose to ground, before urination and defecation. In dogs restricted in small pens urination and defecation occur in one specific place; this specificity develops between four and five weeks of age.

Turn around and smell feces or urine after elimination (immature dogs may ingest feces).

Scratching or scraping ground with all four feet after elimination—occasionally in female. This may be a marking activity (especially seen when one dog is in high tension owing to the presence of another strange dog or adversary).

Male:

Running with female.

Sniffs and licks anogenital area.

"Tongues" after testing female's urine or genitalia, the tongue being curled slightly and the tip rapidly and repeatedly pushed upward behind the front incisors (possibly stimulating the organs of Jacobson).

May urinate nearby and scrape after urinating.

Play-wrestling.

Forepaws extended, body thrown back on haunches, head to one side (play-soliciting).

Tail and ears erect, stands squarely in front or to one side of female (display).

Pushes against female with neck, shoulder or hip.

Places neck or forefoot onto shoulder or back of female (may rest perpendicular to female with head on her shoulder, forming a T position).

Licks or nibbles shoulder and neck of female.

Mounting.

Clasping with forelimbs (occasionally grips neck of female with teeth, Fuller and DuBuis, 1962).

Pelvic thrusts.

Copulatory tie.

Female:

Running with male.

Sniffs and licks anogenital area.

Play-wrestling.

Forepaws extended, body thrown back on haunches, head to one side (play-soliciting).

Submissive.

Stands for male and allows mounting (if at right phase of heat).

Tail placed to one side and vulva displayed.

May mount male, clasp and show pelvic thrusts.

Ingestive Behavior:

Sucking, butting with head and kneading with forefeet, and pushing with hind feet, with tail out and down (in neonate only).

Lapping, tail out and down.

Chewing and swallowing, tail out and down.

Gnawing and pulling, holding food with forefeet.

Eating grass.

Hunting Behavior (includes *exploratory* and *aggressive* behavior

Stalking and pointing (piloerection rare).

Herding.

Digging (when prey goes to ground).

Shaking, throwing, catching and killing.

Prey-carrying.

Prey-guarding (aggressive behavior against peers).

Prey-burying (food cache).

Play Behavior:

This complex behavioral system is comprised of several patterns of other systems of behavior which through play become elaborated and organized. Component patterns of exploratory, social-investigative, alleomimetic, (et-epimeletic,) agonistic sexual and hunting behavior can be recognized. Play-soliciting gestures appear exaggerated and include pawing, with wide eyes and pricked ears; growling and barking; tail erect and wagged; hindquarters higher than forequarters, head low, occasionally moved from side to side; approaches with hindquarters higher, as in a crawl-walk or in short pounces or jumps, and may withdraw in a similar pattern—i.e., exaggerated approach-withdrawal ambivalence.

Socialization Processes in the Dog

Age in Weeks	1 2 3	4 5 6 7	8 9 10 11	12 13 14 15
Behavior	Neonatal and Transitional Periods	Onset of Socialization Period	Weaning	
Relationships	Maternal feeding and shelter	Interaction with peers and Environment	Play. Exploration.	Dominant-subordinate relationships . . . .
Proccesses	Nurture	Approach behavior Unstable learning	Avoidance behavior Stable learning	Socialization complete
Variables	Prenatal influences and genetic factors			Early experience
Dog Human Relations	. . . . Too "human dependent"	. . . . Optimum age for socialization with both dog and man		. . . . Too "dog attached"

Appendix II

Answers to Some Common Canine Questions

THE FOLLOWING QUESTIONS have been appended because they represent some of the most commonly occurring problems that dog owners and breeders have presented to the author over the past several years. For convenience they have been arbitrarily divided into three general categories—developmental problems, general behavior questions and problems concerning abnormal and undesirable traits.

Developmental Problems

Can there be problems, and if so what, when there is only one pup in a litter? Shouldn't it have playmates its own age?

There can be serious problems if the bitch is afraid of human beings, for the pup might also pick up this trait. The bitch may be aggressive and excessively assert her dominance over the pup, and this too may be detrimental. She may not be very playful and interact little with the pup, and this could be very bad for it is important for the pup to interact a good deal with his own kind as well as with people—otherwise his socialization will be inadequate. When pups play together they learn to inhibit the bite and they also develop a social hierarchy which is an important aspect of social adjustment. Without these experiences, the pup might grow up into an uninhibited, hard-biting, socially maladjusted delinquent. Very much as with children, it is important that the pup be socialized with its own peer group. This would also "buffer" or dilute any undesirable characteristics that might be acquired from the parents (or bitch, in your case). Your puppy should be put in a canine "kibbutz" school as soon as he is weaned, and if the bitch is a really bad mother, wean the pup early. Colonel R. Weaver of the Scottish Terrier Club of America tells me that one of his Scotties is a "super mother" because she will play with her pups quite roughly until they stand up for themselves. This brings out a lot of confidence and spunk in them. He uses this bitch to "terrierize" offspring of a more placid, easygoing bitch. This is a most intriguing point to consider, where the mother's behavior has a clear influence on her offsprings' behavioral development.

You have put a lot of weight on the importance of socializing pups during the critical socialization period which you say is from about four until twelve weeks of age. Now, I followed your instructions to the letter and yet my schnauzer started to get very spooky at around five months and he's been that way ever since. Explain please!

I, too, am facing the identical problem with a very find coyote-dog hybrid that was well socialized during the critical period. Suddenly at around four and a half months, she started to show fear and flight reactions to sudden noises and even more violent reactions to some alteration in her familiar environment, say, a box placed in the middle of the room or a cupboard left open that's usually kept closed. I have seen this same fear developing at this age in wolves, coyotes and jackals, and I feel that in many domesticated dogs this developmental aspect of the wild temperament has been bred out and a more stable temperament has been selected for. Even so, some dogs may manifest some of the traits of their wild ancestors. Indeed the temperament or nervous typology of dogs does not mature until twelve or eighteen months, and there may be many unstable periods during this time which behavior research in this country has not yet identified. The Russians, using Pavlovian conditioning tests, claim to have identified such periods and their work in this area is really very advanced.

My sixteen-month-old terrier has started growling at people and I have tried everything to inhibit this. I want to show him: He goes to people for petting and is affectionate but still growls. This started soon after he was used as a stud. Is this just a stage he will grow out of, and what can I do to speed up its departure?

This may well be a phase that your now sexually mature dog is going through. He is testing the reactions of others, just as he would another dog. If a person or dog stands his ground and doesn't trigger your dog to assert his dominance or to lose face, then the behavior should give way to an indifferent standoff or overt friendliness. Discipline, I feel, would only make a terrier more aggressive. At this stage he is testing how far he can go, and if his growls are ignored and literally smothered in confident affection and not encouraged or reinforced by discipline or withdrawal, they should disappear. The possibility that he may become even more "egocentric" or aggressively intolerant of the close proximity of others should also be borne in mind. If this is the case, he should be culled from your breeding stock if severe choke-chain discipline does not work. But do not resort to severe discipline unless he becomes more aggressive.

I want to buy a pup but I already have a dog. What is the best way to introduce the new pup so as not to make the older dog fight or feel jealous?

First, you might introduce the two on neutral territory—somewhere where neither has been before. This way your older dog might not feel that his home territory is being violated. He may tolerate and even play with the youngster and accept him readily when you return home. Try meeting a friend in the park; you have your dog and your friend arrives with your pup. Then return home, your friend coming in a few minutes later with your pup. Give your older dog lots of attention, petting, tidbits, and so on. Really make him feel good, otherwise he may become quite aggressive or neurotic if he senses that his relationship with you is being threatened. Allow him to growl and dominate the young pup—up to a point—for it is quite natural for him to assert his dominance. To punish him for displaying his superiority would be cruel. But if he starts to get rough, then a verbal reprimand before more severe discipline would be called for.

My puppy chews up and eats all kinds of things. Is this because he has worms?

Your pup might coincidentally have worms. You should arrange with your veterinarian to have the dog checked. It is, however, quite normal for pups to investigate, sniff, chew and swallow a wide variety of objects. This is part of the exploratory behavior of young pups, an essential component of learning what things are, how they taste and smell and whether or not they are edible. They will also chew a good deal when they are teething, especially at around four months of age—just like human infants. Pups can, however, get into trouble with sharp or splintering objects which may perforate some part of the digestive tract. Others may get a blockage when a foreign body gets stuck in the small intestine. You should provide your pup with such chewable play objects as a marrow bone or the rawhide or rubber bones that most pet stores carry. Watch out for electrical cords, though. More than one pup has received severe burns and shock after chewing through a live cord.

My puppy chases his tail like mad and I have to stop him or else he gets dizzy and falls over. Is this normal?

This is sometimes normal, but it *can* be a sign that something is irritating him. Pups will do this when they are excited and in a playful mood, and we call this self-play. The tip of the tail seems to be an elusive object—possibly resembling prey—that catches the corner of the dog's eye and stimulates him to twist around and chase it. The more he whirls, the faster he has to chase it. Literally a vicious circle! Tail chasing can also stem from excessive confinement, however. The animal has nothing else to do. When a confined dog is released from his kennel, he may be hyperaroused and engage in tail chasing or a "whirling fit." This has been reported experimentally in isolation-raised Scottish terriers. Tail chasing and biting may also be due to anal gland irritation or nervous irritation at a docked tail. The dog is usually more anxious then and may really mutilate himself.

I take young pups to shows before they are old enough to go into the ring to "shape" them up. Often I take a pair, and one does fine where the other goes shy. Why is this and what can I do to prevent it?

I commend you on the excellent procedure of getting your pups used to dog shows before they actually go into the ring, either with you or with a handler. Pups from the same litter rarely have the same genetic constitution or temperament, so it is not surprising that some will be afraid. They have to learn to overcome their fears, and there is no better way than to give them plenty of human contact, "gentling," food reward and also the company of confident dogs. Any occurrence such as the pup's being psychologically traumatized by being too near loudspeakers or accidentally trodden on or threatened or even attacked by another dog can bring on a generalized show phobia. Then you have to go through the protracted procedure of desensitizing by gently handling the dog and slowly exposing him for increasing periods to the show environment. Tranquilizers such as chlorpromazine may be useful, too. Be mindful of the potential hazards of bringing your pups out too soon, however, especially during the "fear periods" at around eight weeks and four and a half to five months of age. It is during such periods of emotional instability that the pup is extremely perceptive and sensitive to changes in his environment and you should avoid exposing the dog to any potentially traumatic conditions at these times. Some pups cope well, while others in the litter, the less stable more nervous individuals, can be more or less permanently affected by bad experiences during these "sensitive" periods.

I want my male shepherd pup castrated so he will be more docile. What's the best age, and will he get too fat?

So far as we know, castration only has a fifty-fifty chance of making an aggressive adult dog more docile. The male sex hormone, testosterone, increases aggressive tendencies and readiness to fight over territory and retaliate against discipline or domination. If the testicles are removed before they begin to produce testosterone, say prior to five months of age, then the chances of arresting the appearance of hormone-related aggressiveness would be greater—greater than waiting until full sexual maturity, for once triggered by testosterone, some aggressive habits may be permanent.

To be most effective, castration should be done at around three months, although it is possible that for 100 percent effectiveness the operation should be performed during the first or second week. It should be remembered that if a young dog is not socialized correctly and does not receive the proper discipline early in life, it may attempt to dominate its owners and may react violently when discipline is attempted. Castration may be of little help under such circumstances.

Some dogs do become obese after castration and occasionally attain large proportions. Often, though these changes are caused by improper diet and inadequate exercise.

In England there has been much correspondence in the veterinary literature concerning dog castration. For house pets this should be seriously considered, in order to reduce the population of dogs in rural and urban areas. City pounds in both America and England are forced to destroy hundreds of thousands of surplus dogs annually. One way to reduce this population explosion is to legally enforce owners to have their dogs castrated if they are not pedigreed or are not intended to be used for stud purposes. The same holds true for bitches—a more expensive operation, but no less essential in dealing with a pathetic surplus of unwanted dogs and the unnecessary suffering of homeless animals prior to humane destruction.

How do children and dogs compare in their development? Do pups go through similar stages to children?

There are, indeed, many similarities in the development of child and dog. The main difference, however, lies in the fact that the child is perceptually mature (in that it can see and hear) long before its locomotor system has developed. In contrast, the dog does not show this sensory-motor division. Its sensory abilities develop more in synchrony with its locomotor abilities. Both pup and child have a critical period for socialization, which begins

Comparative Stages of Development in Dog and Man

Period	Approximate age limits		Behavior
	Dog	Man	
Neonatal	0-2 weeks	0-5 weeks	Dependent on mother for food and care.
Transitional	2-3½ weeks	Not present	Period of rapid sensory and motor development.
Primary Socialization	3½-12 weeks	5 weeks-7 months	Formation of emotional attachments; smiling (man) and tail wagging, denotes presence of fear period in dog and man, at approximately 8 weeks and 8 months respectively.
Transition 1	Not present in dog	7-15 months	Transition to adult methods of eating and walking, denotes presence of fear period in dog and man, at approximately 8 weeks and 8 months respectively.
Transition 2	Not present in dog	15-27 months	Transition to adult talking.
Juvenile	12 weeks-sexual maturity	Equivalent to verbal socialization period in man-27 months-7 or 8 years	Perfection of motor skills and communication.

around two months in the child and around four weeks in the
dog. Both pup and child show a fear period during this
socialization time, which peaks in the dog at around eight weeks
and in the human infant at around eight to nine months. The
different stages of development shown in the accompanying
table are taken from the work of Dr. J. P. Scott, who has contributed a great deal to our understanding of both canine and
human development.

General Behavior

*Can a dog (domestic) and a wolf reproduce together? Also, my
twelve-week-old German shepherd puppy wets the ground when
he comes to me after I call him. Why should he show this fear?
He also shows minor signs of submission such as lowering ears
and slightly wagging his tail, etc. What should I do to make him
much more happy about coming?*

A male wolf will crossbreed with a dog, and a she-wolf will
accept a male dog; such crossbreeding is facilitated by raising
and socializing the wolf with dogs from an early age.

There is nothing fearful about your pup's urination. It's a
normal part of submission, and young dogs frequently do this to
superior dogs and to people. Don't punish him for urinating
because he's only showing his affection and deference for you.
With time he will mature out of this.

Some dogs do urinate, defecate and even empty their anal
glands when they are terrified, but in your case there is no need
to suspect that your pup is unduly timid or that he does not enjoy
approaching you when called. He's just a normal, well-adjusted,
sociable little pup!

*Our fifteen-month-old male Shetland sheep dog never licks our
faces to show his affection or when he's excited about something.
Instead he nibbles at our hair much in the same way he does in
stopping an itch on himself. How unusual is this, what could
have caused such a deviation and how can we discourage this
hair biting?*

My dog has a habit of cleaning my family's hair. She cleans my bangs and also my mother's hair every morning when she comes to wake her up. She also cleans her doll's hair every night between 8 and 8:30 P.M. What causes her to do this?

It is certainly unusual for your dog never to lick your face, although the nibbling "flea biting" is in itself a normal behavior. Dogs do it to each other as a part of intense greeting, and I have seen male dogs "courting" females engaging in a good deal of scruff-oriented nibbling. My coyotes and wolves greet me with a combination of licking, nibbling and seizing my hand or chin in their jaws. The high frequency of your dog's nibbling is probably due to some inhibition of the normal licking and its replacement by the social "nibble-grooming." Why this has occurred I have no idea. I would avoid bending down to your dog, and possibly when he can no longer reach your hair (which releases the nibbling response) he may start to lick and gently mouth an extended hand instead.

A very similar situation may exist in the second question, where the dog engages in this social nibble-grooming. This may be combined with licking, or licking-washing can occur separately. Again there is a strong possibility that hair releases this grooming behavior, much in the same way a bitch will groom and lick her pups dry and then continue to groom and clean them. Dogs, wolves, gray foxes and coyotes all engage in social grooming as adults. I have a red fox that was housed with two jackals, and she would groom (nibble and lick) their eyelids for extended periods. I had to separate them because the jackals eventually lost all the hair around their eyes. They obviously enjoyed this attention, but they looked as though they had hangovers! You may recall visiting the zoo and seeing the monkeys grooming each other. They are not picking fleas off (although they will occasionally eat dead scales of skin). This behavior, as in the canines, is an important aspect of their social interaction.

My ten-month-old German shepherd became very upset when a mentally retarded person entered the room. She stiffened up and went into a barking fit. She is normally quiet and doesn't pay attention to people who come in. Do dogs have a sixth sense? I see no other reason for her behavior.

I would not say that your shepherd has any sixth sense. Dogs are extremely perceptive of subtle nonverbal cues, such as the way in which a person moves, stands, if he is tense, relaxed, fidgety and anxious, confident and smooth-moving, nervously staring at the dog, and so on. This is why a dog can quickly tell if a person is afraid of him or not. Dogs communicate with each other mainly through the nonverbal silent body language described in Chapter 9, so that they are especially aware of subtle body movements and postures.

Your mentally retarded visitor most probably had some fine defect in his actions and behavior—be it in the tone of voice, body posture, movement, facial expression or eye contact—that really disturbed the dog. This visitor did not fit the expectancy model that your dog had built up about people.

Schizophrenics apparently may have an unusual odor, and it is quite possible that the dog will detect this (it has been shown that rats, and some psychiatrists, are very sensitive to this odor) and behave warily, defensively or even aggressively.

People without such emotional handicaps, but having a limp, outlandish costume or black skin in a white neighborhood (and vice versa) can similarly disturb dogs by their novelty and minor unfamiliar idiosyncracies of behavior. The stealth and other unusual behaviors of a sneaking burglar are enough to turn on the most placid dog. The experienced burglar would always try to behave as normally as possible. If his behavior makes him appear unsuspicious, then neigher dog nor policeman might intercept.

After watching obedience trials and in training my own dog, I get the impression that most dogs respond better to hand signals than to voice commands. What does this difference mean and how general is it?

Part of your question is answered in the previous one. Dogs are very perceptive of body movements and it is primarily via body signals that dogs communicate with each other. It is logical therefore that they should readily learn a number of hand signals. The trouble is the variety of clear arm and hand signals that are effective at a distance is limited, so that additional vocal commands may greatly increase the repertoire. To make the point clearer, we have a far more elaborate vocal than arm signal repertoire; some well-trained dogs can respond to over fifty different vocal commands. Additional cues can be given by the trainer's eyes, and a well-trained dog is literally "all eyes" on its trainer.

Do dogs dream, like us?

Dogs certainly do dream, and we can guess a little about the content of their dreams by watching them. We hear growls, whimpers, whines, muffled barks, and see the tail wagging or the legs making running movements. Some male dogs have been said to ejaculate. Other dogs may urinate while asleep. When a recording of brain wave activity is made during quiet sleep and while dreaming, the waves change from big and slow in quiet sleep to small and fast in dreaming. This latter activity pattern is much like the state of wakefulness, and we find almost identical patterns in man. Dreaming is called activated, paradoxical or rapid eye movement (REM) sleep by neurophysiologists and is seen in all mammals, including cats, dogs, monkeys and men. Why animals and man have to dream remains a mystery yet to be explained by science.

I have read Man Meets Dog *by Konrad Lorenz and he says that some dogs have a jackal ancestry and others have more wolf blood. Is this true?*

Since the publication of his book, Professor Lorenz has changed his views in line with current thinking about the origin of the dog. It is now generally agreed, but not definitely proven, as described in Chapter I, that the wolf is the main if not sole ancestor of the dog. The domesticated dog is buried under at least 10,000 years of human history, and we will probably never be really sure about its ancestry and origin or multiple origins.

Possibly the Asiatic wolf (*Canis lupus pallipes*) is the grandfather of them all. Future studies in behavior and genetics of various wild members of the canine family may lead us closer to the answer.

Do dogs scratch after evacuating to cover up what they have done like cats? Mine never does.

No, dogs do not have an atrophied or incomplete pattern of covering their urine and feces. Their behavior is in no way related to that of the cat. What dogs are doing is marking the earth by scraping with the hind and forelegs. This serves as an additional signal in their deposition of calling cards in their territory. A dog will often only scrape when he sees another dog approaching or when he is near the home of a rival. Wild animals such as panthers also use their urine to mark their territory and will scrape the tree against which they have urinated with their claws.

I have two male dogs—Kerry blues—that have been wanting to fight it out for months now. They live in [adjacent rooms] and I am afraid that one day they are going to kill each other. Please advise.

This is a difficult and all too common problem, and you have a pretty aggressive breed, too. With some breeds, like their wolf ancestors, fighting stops as soon as one rolls over submissively. But in some breeds, especially the terriers, the weaker dog may continue to fight until he is nearly dead. Occasionally the stronger dog will continue to attack even when his adversary has surrendered. Selective breeding in some dogs seems to have severely influenced the ritualistic controls that normally operate during conflict and which tend to reduce the possibility of severe physical injury.

I suggest that you first let the dogs get together on neutral territory, say some park area where neither dog has ever been before. Keep each on the leash, each dog being controlled by a separate handler. It is possible that they might make a peace treaty and not feel the need to fight to defend their territories as they do at home in adjacent runs.

When you get home, you might risk letting them fight it out: That is entirely up to you. A powerful hose should be handy to douse them with. But don't interrupt the fight too early. This is done too often by people, and both dogs get even more frustrated and eager to fight and to work out which one is dominant—just like children. Let the dogs fight it out within reason. Once one is clearly the loser, then pull them apart if the loser continues to fight or the winner does not turn off.

The fact that the dogs are in [adjacent cages] will also increase their territorial rivalry. A more conservative remedy would be to put a solid partition between them or to house them in different runs so that they cannot see each other. They will be less likely to challenge each other, and their mutual feelings of animosity might well be extinguished.

We plan to breed our elkhound bitch with a male wolf and feel that it would result in a dog having the best characteristics of both parents. What do you think? Also how would the male wolf we get do as a pet?

What you will most probably have in the hybrid litter will be a number of pups that have some of the wild temperament of the wolf. This undesirable temperament includes overfearfulness of unfamiliar objects and people and overreactivity which is seen as a violent flight reaction to changes in the animal's familiar environment. A table moved to a new place or a cardboard package on the living-room floor can evoke flight before the animal cautiously investigates. Contrast this kind of temperament with the average dog: He would probably not show any overt reaction if you had moved the table, and with the package he would immediately investigate it and soon have it undone. Some wolf hybrids have a very stable temperament, but many will begin to show these wild traits at around four and a half to five months of age. It is quite possible that when such an overreactive animal is cornered or his flight is blocked by some obstacle or person, he might momentarily bite out of fear. And a fear-biter of such size and speed is a most unreliable animal to have around. He would be safe if you could guarantee a stable environment—no changes, no strangers and *predictably* behaving children and adults. You can, however, rarely rely on the latter with absolute confidence, for children and adults who begin to get to know an animal well will often forget that it is wild, is potentially dangerous or has a need for privacy.

The above remarks hold true for pure wolves, too. I would not recommend one as a pet. Even if you did get one that had a stable temperament, transient changes occur during the breeding season—the animal may become more aggressive to strangers—dog or human. As a house pet, a wolf is out. He is so active and exploratory—into everything far more than a three-year-old child. A sofa might be dug out one night for a den, and "safe" things placed high on a dresser or mantelpiece will eventually be reached. No, a wolf will never become a pet. In a large outdoor enclosure with other wolves or dogs with whom he has been raised, a hand-reared wolf will do well, provided he is always treated with respect. And for this he will return affection and give you something far deeper in his relationship with you than you have probably ever experienced with any other dog or wild animal before.

I have a bitch that raises one leg like a male to urinate. Is there something wrong with her hormones? She has normal heats.

It is unusual but not abnormal for bitches to urinate in this way. Many of the dog's wild cousins—golden jackals, bush dogs and red foxes, for example—will do this or even do a handstand and urinate with both hind feet off the ground. It is more unusual for male dogs *not* to cock a hind leg to urinate. This may be due to delayed sexual maturation or be a consequence of castration early in life. In groups of dogs—or wolves—penned together, subordinate males may be socially inhibited from raising one leg. Only the leader or a couple of top-rank males show the mature pattern. Occasionally an adult male dog may begin to urinate in the female pattern and, indeed, he may attract other males by his odor and they may show a good deal of sexual interest in him. I have seen a few dogs like this, and they invariably had a tumor on the testicle, a Sertoli cell tumor, which as it grows begins to secrete increasing amounts of the female sex hormone estrogen. This makes the male behave in a more female manner, and he may even begin to look more female as his teats become larger and his rump fatter!

My bitch schnauzer grins like a human being—a kind of half snarl, half smile—only when she is with people and when she is greeting them. Some of her offspring do this, too, although none in another litter from another schnauzer who doesn't grin do this. Am I right in thinking this is genetic?

At the turn of the century, Charles Darwin in *The Origin of Expressions and Emotions in Man and Animal* described this canine grin, which does resemble the canine snarl but which is invariably directed at human beings. It may be a social response that some dogs are capable of mimicking from human beings. I think that you are right that the ability to turn on this expression may well be inherited, but the extent to which early learning contributes to this inherited ability remains to be determined. I have heard of a West Coast veterinarian whose Doberman pinscher "grinned." With a penchant for dental work, he put gold caps on the dog's front teeth to enhance the dog's display! This canine grin that is analogous to the human grin should be differentiated from the submissive grin that is seen in all canines, where the lips are retracted horizontally and the teeth are not bared. This is analogous to the human smile, occurring when a dog meets and greets a socially superior canine or human being.

I have some great Scottish terriers, but when they go into the ring they keep looking at me and telling me they are trying their best. In so doing they keep flattening their ears, which just won't get them any points. Please advise.

First I would ask if you have earlier either overindulged or excessively dominated your terriers so that they are too dependent or too subordinate. Second, I wonder if you have a more submissive but not necessarily timid strain. I personally feel that a dog should not lose points for showing such deference to his owner or handler, and I wonder what kinds of temperaments are being unwittingly selected for in those show dogs that consistently maintain an alert "ready to go" posture in the show ring. Some are being alerted by tidbits of food or by the handler's pretending to eat. Others may be more confident and aggressive and temperamentally unsuitable for anything else *but* the show ring. Still others may be "zombies" that as a consequence of genetic selection and training will stay obediently in one "alert" position for hours. They might be useful outside the show ring as apartment or lawn ornaments, but for little else!

They say dogs are color-blind, but my dog seems to prefer my child's red ball and red shoes over similar objects of a different color. Is it possible for him to see colors, then?

So far as we know, dogs are unable to distinguish colors. Different colors of the same intensity are equally gray to the dog. The dog is color-blind. All colors to him are varying shades of gray, ranging from black through white: Everything is in monochrome. But the dog's retina is very sensitive to movement, and this sensitivity, coupled with a keen nose and ear, more than compensates for his color-blindness and makes him a very efficient hunter.

Why your dog prefers one colored ball over another may be related to its size, taste, smell or perhaps it is your perceptual bias, for *you* may be more likely to notice him with the red ball than, say, with a black or brown one—and all the more so if the red one is your child's favorite!

How can I stop my dog rolling in all kinds of unmentionable stuff? He comes in smelling worse than a skunk, and as soon as I bathe him, he's out again and comes back stinking.

Your dog is doing what comes naturally. Dogs seem to have an esthetic appreciation of odors, much as we have of music or the gourmet of his aged meat and cheese. The only suggestion that I can offer is to keep your dog tethered in the yard so that he can't go off and indulge his olfactory sense. Punishment is of little value, for how can the dog know that he has done wrong when what he does is natural! If he likes human perfumes, you might try putting a little on him, on each side of his throat and behind his ears. He might then be content, although some dogs after such treatment or after being bathed with perfumed soap will immediately run off and find something to roll in, perhaps to mask their perfumed aura. I repeat, you are facing a problem of instinctual behavior, and that's well-nigh impossible to inhibit.

My spaniel likes to eat salads (without too much dressing!)and sometimes he will eat grass. Is this normal for a meat-eater or is it because he's been domesticated?

No, his behavior is not a consequence of domestication. It is quite normal for carnivores (flesh-eating mammals) to eat various herbs and grasses. On a pure meat diet, as has been discovered in zoos, carnivores may die or develop a deformed skeleton. In nature, they eat the viscera, the stomach and intestinal contents of their prey, which contain much vegetable matter rich in vitamins and trace elements. They may also get these essential substances directly from certain plants.

Dogs will often vomit after eating grass, and a few round worms may also be thrown up. Did they eat the grass to induce vomiting, or does the more fibrous grass irritate the stomach lining and accidentally cause vomiting? We really don't know, although my own animals will eat, and hold down, more tender grass and throw up with apparent ease and without having eaten any grass to induce it. It is a good idea for people living in apartments to grow a little grass for their cat: Perhaps a "house bound" dog might also enjoy such a vegetarian treat, provided he does not decide to throw everything up afterward.

Once again my bitch is coming into heat and I don't want all the dogs in the neighborhood around. Help, please!

After she has had her heat, please consider having her spayed. So many bitches eventually get bred unintentionally, and if you never intend to breed her, it would save you a lot of trouble and also contribute to lowering the population crisis of stray dogs in both rural and urban areas. In many rural areas they are crossbreeding with wild coyotes, and the offspring remain wild and are more fertile than coyotes (having two instead of one heat per year), so that the population of feral or wild "coydogs" is becoming a serious problem in many areas.

To stop dogs coming a-courting you must look to the calling card your bitch is leaving for them. One part of her urine diluted a million parts in water can still be picked up by a dog when she is in heat, because it contains a special chemical or pheromone which she only normally produces at this time. She should be taken out in the car to a distant park or kept in the yard if you have one secure enough to keep away her suitors. Some people claim that chlorophyll tablets given orally will mask her urine signal, but a safer way is to get a "contraceptive injection" from your veterinarian. I personally do not favor such hormone injections for they can have undesirable side effects in some individuals. Spaying is far safer but cannot be done until the heat period is over, for hemorrhage during surgery can occur if the operation is performed while she is still in heat.

Abnormal and Undesirable Traits

My shepherd spooked the other day when I came in wearing a new hat. In fact, it's the first hat I've worn in years. He barked and growled for some time before he seemed to know who I was. Is this unusual in dogs?

No, this is not unusual. At a certain distance they will rely not on scent or voice cues but on visual cues as to your identity, and any unusual alteration of your dress would make your dog respond as he did. I have a coyote who intensely dislikes human females, and he seems to rely on smell at close proximity and on visual cues at a greater distance. Thus he will accept the approach of females who have short hair and who are wearing jeans but threatens them suddenly when they are close to him. Long-haired males in bell-bottom pants will be threatened at a distance but accepted when he has smelled them! Animals seem to respond at a certain distance to a whole complex of stimuli or gestalt. Some seem less able to separate familiar from unfamiliar components. Thus a bull, who was as docile as a lamb with its handler, one day viciously attacked him. The bull seemed not to recognize the handler on that fateful day, for he was wearing, instead of the usual brown work coat, a white coat because the bull was to be shown at the local agricultural fair.

Does chaining a dog up make it more aggressive?

It is certainly true that when one approaches a dog that is chained up, it will invariably put on a great show of aggression or territorial defense by barking and lunging at you. It may also attempt to bite. Often the "front end" of such a dog is showing aggression, while the "hind end" is friendly; the tail wags furiously while the face is aggressive. A dog kept on such a restricted personal territory, may, as suggested by the famous zoo psychologist Heini Hediger, develop a "hypertrophy" of values so that its territorial defensive behavior becomes abnormally intense. Often when such a dog is unchained, it is very friendly outside its own personal territory, but if the chain accidentally breaks while the dog is defending his territory against an intruder, the latter, be it dog or man, may be chased and even attacked.

I have a three-year-old mongrel that started at about one year to show fear of thunder and rain when it hit the gutters of the house. Her fright is now complete terror—any noise like thunder or rain upsets her. She runs around and even jumps on my lap. What do I do for her, especially when I'm out of the house during a storm?

Your dog's phobia is a very common one. A colleague, Dr. Ferdinand Brunner of Vienna, has treated many such cases and claims good results by using tranquilizers. Dogs can tell when a storm is brewing; they are probably very sensitive to changes in barometric pressure. Your veterinarian could prescribe a suitable tranquilizer such as chlorpromazine or any of the phenothiazine derivatives. The dose should be sufficient to quiet the dog but not to make him uncoordinated. Under the right fear-blocking drug, he may learn to overcome his phobia.

Another possible treatment is to make a good tape-recording of thunder and rain and to play the tape at various times especially when the dog is hungry. Encourage him with kind words, petting and tidbits. This reward in the face of what he fears may gradually desensitize him and his phobia will disappear.

My six-month-old German shepherd is very distrustful of strangers, although he is not a "fear-snapper." He growls and barks at strangers in the house but makes up to them if they squat down. Then he growls and barks again when they get up. He is fearful outdoors when approaching large objects such as trucks or buses. Is this a sign of poor temperament or is it simply the German shepherd aloofness that I've heard so much about?

Distrust of strangers is a good and normal trait in the guard dog shepherd type. Fear-biting is something else. It seems that the good quality of wariness in your dog is combined with what I call the wild dog trait of extreme wariness, bordering on fear of strangers and of large or novel stimuli. He may grow out of this by one to one and a half years or with sexual maturity become increasingly aggressive. If you don't intend to use him for breeding, I suggest castration, plus disciplinary training. You must be the boss and control the aggressive reactions that may appear as he matures. But if he does not grow out of this fear phase, the prognosis is not good. He may really have a wild dog temperament and the end result may well be humane destruction or finding him a foster home out in the unchanging countryside on a farm or rural homestead.

How do I stop my dog from chasing kids on their bikes? He points them and then rushes, barking at the back wheels, and though he won't bite anyone, he might make a child fall off a bike and get hurt.

Your dog is doing what comes naturally, but to an unnatural stimulus. A moving object—be it a ball, a running cat or a bicycle wheel—releases the prey-chasing and sometimes the prey-attack response which is part of the dog's innate propensity. This is a difficult response to inhibit because it is a very strong ingrained reaction. One method is to get the children to bicycle around and check your dog with a verbal command followed by a tug on a choke chain. If after repeated trials this does not work, you could give the children water pistols. A couple of squirts in the dog's face might be a very effective and permanent deterrent after only a few trials.

My dog eats his droppings. What can I do to stop it?
This is a very common and disagreeable vice (called coprophagia), especially in kennel housed dogs. In pets, various things can be tried. First, get him out on the leash and while he is defecating try to discreetly pour kerosene onto his stools and then allow him to turn around and attempt to eat them. A few trials should inhibit him pretty fast.

Some authorities feel that the dog may have a nutritional deficiency. Some animals, such as rabbits, normally eat their feces in order to obtain certain B vitamins which are formed by bacteria in fresh feces. Adding a few pieces of raw liver to the dog's diet may help. If all else fails, you might get some capsules, such as butyric acid, from your veterinarian. These will, when digested by your dog, give the stools a very unpleasant taste, which may be sufficient to break the vice.

My dog turned and bit my three-year-old who was near his food bowl while he was eating. He had tooth marks on his cheeks. Will the dog get worse and should I put him to sleep now, just in case?
No, don't put him to sleep yet! If the child gets worse, the bites might get worse. Teach your child to respect the dog. He has certain needs, especially for privacy, a place where he can retire and feel safe, to eat and sleep. It sounds as if you have a good dog. His bite was clearly *inhibited*. If he really meant harm, one bite would put your child in the hands of the surgeon.

Both my wife and I go out to work and our dog barks a lot and makes a mess in the house. How can we stop this?
Dogs are social animals, and when we take them as pets we are

substituting ourselves in the place of dogs that would normally be his pack companions. It is really inhumane to keep a dog "in solitary" all day. Many couples who go out to work realize this and eventually get rid of their dogs.

One possible remedy is to get the pet a pet! Rather than purchasing another dog, a companion cat or even a box turtle has more than once served as a miraculous cure for the social needs of the dog. Excessive barking and destructive tendencies in the home disappear overnight.

I am a reading specialist working with children with various problems including severe emotional ones. These children might benefit from having a pet of their own, but I'm always afraid that because a child's problems often stem from the home situation, a pet might really suffer in the same situation. What do you think? I do feel that a dog can be made neurotic by human contact—or am I being overanalytical?

As yet no studies have been done to determine to what degree home environment contributes to a dog's developing some abnormality in behavior. Certainly the way in which the dog is raise—overindulged, permissively, overdominated, and so—can drastically alter its behavior.

A timid dog would naturally fare worse in a noisy, turbulent household than would a more stable dog. In some households, the social structure is such that the dog is a bystander and is in no way a part of (and is therefore not influenced by) any social and emotional disturbances. In other cases, the dog could be very much involved as a target for the redirected frustrations and aggression of one or more individuals or, conversely, an emotional support and source of affection for a child or adult in a troubled household. Dr. Boris Levinson has discussed such issues in detail in my book *Abnormal Behavior in Animals* (Saunders, Philadelphia, 1968).

It would be extremely interesting to do a careful study of the behavior of dogs from homes where there are one or more schizophrenic individuals or an autistic or hyperactive child.

I think that all the work that you do for dogs is a waste of time and money. There are so many poor, starving and emotionally sick children in the world. Why don't you help them?

I appreciate your point. I spend some 30 percent of my time in research and it is not *for* dogs but to give us insight and enlightenment about the process of evolution and of the phenomenon of life and of man. By studying the development of behavior and social organization of animals, I hope to identify some of the factors which may impair development and disrupt social organization in both animals in nature and man in his "unnature." I see poverty, starvation and many mental illnesses as consequences of man's emancipation from natural forces which regulate population size and the quality of life. Man has to develop unnatural controls, a new, socially oriented technology, to restore or at least prevent further deterioration of life, from the one-cell organisms in Lake Erie to the termitelike masses of humanity in New York and Calcutta.

Some of my work *does* have practical value for dogs and their owners. Your point about wasting money is no longer true, for government funds for basic research are very limited.

My Dalmatian barks every day at the milk truck and at the laundry van, which is disturbing to my parents and their business. Please advise.

Your dog, in barking especially at the milk and laundry vehicles, is really defending his territory against particular, regular intruders. He undoubtedly knows the approximate time of day when each of these vehicles and their operators come by your home. Other dogs make a big thing of barking, threatening, and sometimes even attacking regular intruders such as mailmen and milkmen. I have walked in some suburban areas where pedestrians are rare, for there is no sidewalk: Everyone drives except delivery men who are probably going to enter the dog's personal territory. And the response that I get is always the same: growls and barks that continue until I have passed one dog's territory and until I enter the next. In England, where in many suburban areas people go on foot, there is far less of this territorial defense reaction in response to strangers, although the habitual intruders, the milkman and the postman, experience the same canine territorial ritual as their American counterparts. To inhibit this behavior is extremely difficult. Verbal and mild physical punishment every time the dog puts on his aggressive display may be effective but could have the opposite effect of arousing him even more. You might get the cooperation of the laundryman and the milkman and ask them to stop their vehicles and feed the dog some tidbit after you have brought him over on the leash. A few repetitions of this might do the trick. Castration may help, especially if all else fails and he becomes even more aggressive.

References and Useful
Books for Further Reading

Burns, M. and Fraser, M. N., *Genetics of the Dog*. London, Oliver & Boyd, 1966.

Fox, M. W., ed., *Abnormal Behavior in Animals*. Philadelphia, W. B. Saunders, 1968.

————, *Behaviour of Wolves, Dogs and Related Canids*. London, Jonathan Cape, 1971.

————, *Canine Behavior*. Springfield, Ill., C. C. Thomas, 1965.

————, *Canine Pediatrics*. Springfield, Ill., C. C. Thomas, 1966.

————, *Integrative Development of Brain and Behavior in the Dog*. Chicago, Univ. of Chicago Press, 1971.

Krushinskii, L. V., *Animal Behavior*. New York, Consultant Bureau, 1962.

Little, C. C., *The Inheritance of Coat Color in Dogs*. Ithaca, N.Y. Cornell Univ. Press, 1957.

Pfaffenberger, C. J. and Scott, J. P., "The Relationship Between Delayed Socialization and Trainability in Guide Dogs." 'Journal of Genetic Psychology, 95: 145-55, 1959.

tress, 1965.Stockard, C. R., *The Genetic and Endocrinic Basis for Differences in Form and Behavior*. Philadelphia, Wistar Institute, 1941.

Scott, J. P. and Fuller, J. J. *Genetics and Social Behavior of the Dog*. Chicago, Univ. of Chicago Press, 1965.

Stockard, C. R., *The Genetic and Endocrinic Basis for Differences in Form and Behavior*. Philadelphis, Wistar Institute, 1941.

231

Index